W9-BTQ-933

Hoofinfeathers

Hooffin feathers

Easy
Fool Proof
Cooking

Chef
Linda
Wadensten

First Edition
First Printing, October 1997
12,500

Copyright 1997 by Dining Endeavors, Inc.
P. O. Box 908
Charlestown, Rhode Island 02813
(401) 788-0766

All rights reserved. No part of this book may be reproduced or transmitted
in any form or by any means, electronic or mechanical, including
photocopying, recording, or by any information storage and retrieval system,
without prior written permission from Dining Endeavors, Inc. and Linda Wadensten.

Library of Congress Number: 97-068515
ISBN: 0-9658178-0-6

Designed and manufactured in the United States of America by
Favorite Recipes® Press
an imprint of

FRP™

2451 Atrium Way
Nashville, Tennessee 37214
1-800-358-0560

Photography: Shane Photography
Book Design: Steve Newman
Project Manager: Judy Jackson
Cover Illustration: Barbara Ball

03 02 01 00 99 98 97   10 9 8 7 6 5 4 3 2 1

Contents

Acknowledgements

*Thanks to all those closest to me, whose encouragement
and help gave me the strength to complete this book and
the desire to see my dreams and aspirations become a reality.
It's a long road to take, but with friends and family
for reassurance, there is an end.*

Preface

*Dining Endeavors, Inc., is dedicated to educating people
of all creeds and cultures about the secrets of cooking.
My mission is to re-shape how people think of cooking and to
teach them the skills and basic knowledge for cooking.
This is particularly important for our children.
We must give our children the knowledge that our
older generation was given by our "Beaver Cleaver" families.
With the increase in two-income families, it's important that
our children learn these skills, at school if not at home.
In today's society it is imperative to know how to cook
for ourselves, certainly in order to know how to survive,
but most importantly to stay fit and healthy. The basics
introduced in this book will teach you how to cook based on
techniques rather than cuisines. Cuisines are no more than
different ingredients used with those techniques.
It is the techniques that remain a constant. This inevitably
leads to my personal goal of changing the way
our professional institutes teach the culinary arts.
By using basic cooking techniques, we are free to unleash
our imagination to create culinary delights through
each creed and culture, thus making cooking
a fun part of daily life—and not a feared essential.*

Introduction

As a young child I was introduced to the world of food by my Swedish grandmother. Mor-Mor always made sure there was something delicious waiting to be eaten; her dishes filled the house with distinctive aromas, telling you it just had to be something mouth-watering good. Hopefully you, the reader, were as fortunate as I was to wake up every morning to something cooking in the kitchen. Fascinated as a youngster, little did I know I was about to begin a lifelong love affair—a path void of prejudice toward culture or nationality, filled with a diversity of flavors, textures, and techniques. There was a wealth of knowledge for my taking and an adventure to begin.

Cooking is a world of few rules and endless limits, and in this world you, the cook, are the all-powerful ruler. With such power in hand, the creation will always be yours. As a dear friend once said to me, "It's a sensual experience to be able to cook." And you know what—she's right. Cooking uses all the senses. We use our sight, smell, taste, touch, and, yes, we may even *hear* that timer going off. Most importantly, those hands, the creator's hands, are the single most important tool in cooking.

Cooking is how I began my journey into adulthood. It was a great way to make money and meet a lot of people while I was going to school. I soon began college, and even there my love for cooking followed me. Discouraged by the cafeteria menu, I often found myself going to the grocery store and cooking in my dorm room. Obviously, I didn't have a kitchen, but between us my roommates and I had a crockpot, microwave, and toaster oven. I had picked up enough knowledge of cooking from my family and working experiences that I turned those few appliances into a facility comparable to the White House kitchen. Once I had conquered the appliances, I soon began having dinners and late-night hors d'oeuvre for roommates and friends. It was there that a fellow student said to me, "Lin, why don't you go to culinary school and get a degree in culinary arts— you're a natural at it." Well, having almost completed a B.S. in marketing, I left and never looked back. It had just never occurred to me to choose something that I enjoyed doing as a career. Now, after several years of education and many years in the hospitality field, I see that it was the most important choice I have ever made.

As an adult, I have had the pleasure (and hardships) of owning my own business in the hospitality field. Mostly I enjoy entertaining, meeting new people, and seeing the amazement in my guests' eyes as they feast on a decadent and delectable masterpiece of prepared foods. Whatever the occasion, there is always something to cook to fit the mood of the moment. I've always felt that cooking is an art of self-expression. Like beauty, it is very personal—it is in the mouth of the chewer, so to speak. What one person might find to be the absolute greatest, another might rate as just mediocre. Cooking is an endless journey to finding the ultimate dish, and there can be hundreds of them.

In this light, work in the kitchen always reminds me of my favorite Robert Frost poem, "The Road Not Taken":

Two roads diverged in a yellow wood,
And sorry I could not travel both
And be one traveler, long I stood
And looked down one as far as I could
To where it bent in the undergrowth;

Then took the other, as just as fair,
And having perhaps the better claim,
Because it was grassy and wanted wear;
Though as for that the passing there
Had worn them really about the same,

And both that morning equally lay
In leaves no step had trodden black.
Oh, I kept the first for another day!
Yet knowing how way leads on to way,
I doubted if I should ever come back.

I shall be telling this with a sigh
Somewhere ages and ages hence:
Two roads diverged in a wood, and I—
I took the one less traveled by,
And that has made all the difference.

I have always felt this poem relates to both my life and my job. The challenge of the unknown has always intrigued me into finding whatever lies at the end. In many ways cooking is like that less-traveled road, and what lies along the path is for you to find and experience. If there is any one thing I hope you get from this book, let it be that there are few rules in cooking. The one thing that remains a constant is that we must always use at least one of our basic cooking techniques to prepare the foods we eat. These techniques are roasting, frying, sautéing, braising, boiling, grilling, baking, and cold cookery.

The one thing that does change continually is the ingredients that make up the dishes we eat. These ingredients are what make up the wide variety of cuisines we eat. Italian, Mexican, Chinese, or whatever it may be, the only difference is the ingredients used. This is what makes cooking so much fun. The ingredients can always change when using the same technique, so one dish can turn into dozens of new dishes by simply adding another ingredient. Cooking is being fearless in the experimentation with ingredients in each technique.

I'd like to think that great chefs never make a mistake—they just create new dishes. But we are human, so keep that pizza delivery number handy, just in case! When you cook, you never stop learning. Each time you prepare a new recipe, you learn something else. The more you test new recipes, the easier it will become for you to apply all that you have learned from other recipes. Soon you, too, will be cooking on your own, using the techniques and changing the ingredients, based on your memory and understanding of cooking and its many combinations. So don't be afraid to try that new recipe you got. If it calls for onions and you don't like them, don't add them—add something else that you *do* like. Remember, you are the gatekeeper. You choose what should be, so go ahead: Don't be afraid; give it a try. The things you'll learn along the way will amaze you. As you, too, develop your own cooking style, may you never go back to the place in the yellow wood where the two roads diverged.

Kitchen Basics

Kitchen Basics

Pictured on overleaf (recipe page numbers can be found in the index):

Lower left corner: Grilled Shrimp Provençal, Grilled Barbecue Pizza, Grilled Sliced Pineapple, Grilled Vegetable Kabobs, Barbecued Ribs with Herbs, Barbecued Chicken with Kick-Your-Butt Barbecue Sauce, Grilled Steaks, Grilled Swordfish, Marinated Grilled Chicken

Upper right corner: Apricot Papaya Chutney, Cran-Apple Chutney, Star Peach Chutney, Perfect Gravy, Harvest Roasted Vegetables, Roasted Fillet of Fish (sea bass), Roast Turkey, Roasted Red Bliss Potatoes, Roasted Sweet Potatoes (a variation of Roasted Red Bliss Potatoes), Roast Duck a l'Orange, Roast Lamb Chops (a variation of Roast Beef), Roast Pork Loin (a variation of Roast Beef), Peach Halves filled with Mint Jelly

All these dishes were prepared using the Grilling, Roasting, and Cold Cookery techniques.

Other dishes are identified as they appear on the remaining chapter openers.

The Fundamentals

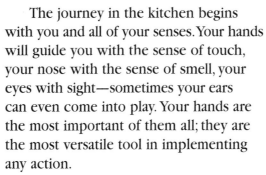

The journey in the kitchen begins with you and all of your senses. Your hands will guide you with the sense of touch, your nose with the sense of smell, your eyes with sight—sometimes your ears can even come into play. Your hands are the most important of them all; they are the most versatile tool in implementing any action.

Of course, good sanitation habits must be applied: **Always** wash your hands before touching food. Hands will tell you if the texture's right; fingers dip into soup to test the temperature, and fingers help taste that soup for just the right seasoning. The sensitivity of your fingers can project an array of impressions about what you are doing. Once you get your fingers in the ingredients, you'll soon recognize if the batter's just the right consistency, if the cake in the oven is baked, if your dough's the right texture, and hundreds more. So, go on—get those hands into the kitchen and *feel* yourself cooking.

The next most important tool is a knife, and I'm not talking about that dull one you picked up at the flea market for a steal—there's a reason it was a steal. The knife will be your closest companion in the kitchen—your best friend and your worst enemy.

First of all, I have to say that you must respect both the nature of any task you undertake and the tools you must use. You should always know the capabilities of your knife and that it can cut you badly. To avoid experiencing the wrath of the blade, be careful and simply respect

its power. And that's no yolking matter (forgive the pun).

Knives will cut, chop, dice, pound, slice, and scrape. Because they're our best friends, we must treat them as such. That means wash your knife in the sink, by hand; never allow it to soak in water or go through the dishwasher. Towel it dry after washing, and always store it alone where the blade is not touching anything else (so it won't become dull). It's a good practice to get frequently used knives sharpened at least twice a year (once a year for knives you don't use daily). Treat your knife like a friend and it will last as long as one.

There are three knives that are crucial to a functioning kitchen. First, there is the chef's knife, which has a long triangular blade. The blades vary in size from 6 to 12 inches; pick one that's comfortable for you. The chef's knife is used for chopping, dicing, mincing, trimming, and scraping. Secondly, there is a slicing knife that has a thin rectangular serrated blade used for slicing anything you'd like, from tomatoes and bread to roasts. Lastly, the paring knife, a miniature of the chef's knife, is used for peeling, mincing, or dicing smaller items, like garlic.

There are many other types of knives you can buy and use, but these three are the absolute basics that you will always need. When you buy knives, go to a reputable kitchen supply house and get good ones. They are not cheap, but if you pay for a good one, it will outlive dozens of the cheap ones. I prefer the knives by Henckels or Dexters.

Now that you have a good knife, the next thing you're going to need is a good cutting board, preferably a wooden one. If you don't use a cutting board, you're likely to damage your knife (and, in most instances, cut yourself).

Timely Tip

Always wash your cutting board thoroughly with hot soapy water after each use to cleanse the board of any harmful bacteria that may have been left behind by the last food cut on it. (This has been the most frequent source of food poisoning cases.) Basically, this means clean it so you don't food poison yourself and everyone else.

Cookware, like knives, should be the best you can afford. The thinner the pan, the easier it will be to burn your dish. This is because thin pans don't distribute heat evenly—thus you get what you pay for. Heavy-duty pans and skillets are what you want to cook all your dishes in. I prefer stainless steel because they seem to cook more evenly and are easier to clean up.

Always start with one of each of these, and if that doesn't seem to be enough, get another. (Remember, you're in control!) My suggestions are a 2-quart saucepan and cover, a 1-quart saucepan, an 8-quart braising pan or oval pot with cover, a 10-inch sauté pan (frying pan), a 6-inch sauté pan, a 12x18x2¹/₂-inch roasting pan, a 9-inch cake pan, a springform pan, and a sheet tray. There are lots of other pans out there, but if you have these, everything else is icing on the cake. If you have the money and space for a lot of cookware, more power to you!

Standard Pan Capacities

When a recipe calls for a particular utensil that you don't have, check the chart below to see what else you could use. If you don't see the exact size you're looking for, use one that's close. You may need to adjust cooking times slightly.

For this capacity	*you could use*
¹/₈ cup	1¹/₂-inch muffin cup
¹/₄ cup	2-inch muffin cup
¹/₃ cup	2¹/₂-inch muffin cup
¹/₂ cup	3-inch muffin cup
⁵/₈ cup	3-inch giant muffin cup
³/₄ cup	6-ounce custard cup
1¹/₄ cups	10-ounce custard cup
2 cups	7-inch pie plate
	2¹/₂x3x5-inch loaf pan
3 cups	8-inch pie plate
	3x4¹/₂x6-inch loaf pan
4 cups (1 quart)	9-inch pie plate
	8-inch round cake pan
	2¹/₂x4x8-inch loaf pan
	1-quart baking dish
	Eight 3-inch muffin cups
	8-inch skillet
	7¹/₂x11³/₄-inch jelly roll pan
5 cups	3¹/₈x4¹/₄x8¹/₂-inch loaf pan

For this capacity	you could use
6 cups (1½ quarts)	1½x8x8-inch square pan
	9-inch round cake pan
	6x10-inch pan
	7-inch tube pan
	3x7½-inch bundt pan
	Twelve 3-inch muffin cups
	10-inch pie plate
8 cups (2 quarts)	9-inch deep-dish pie plate
	2x8x8-inch pan
	7x11-inch pan
	3x5x9-inch loaf pan
	10-inch skillet
9 cups	3x9-inch bundt pan
	3x8-inch tube pan
10 cups (2½ quarts)	9x9-inch pan
	10x15-inch jelly roll pan
11 cups	2x10-inch round cake pan
12 cups (3 quarts)	3x5x11-inch loaf pan
	9-inch angel cake pan
	10-inch tube pan
	3x8-inch springform pan
	3x10½-inch bundt pan
14 cups	12x17-inch jelly roll pan
15 cups	8½x13½-inch pan
	9x13-inch pan
16 cups (4 quarts)	4x10-inch tube pan
	3x9-inch springform pan
	12-inch skillet
18 cups (4½ quarts)	4x10-inch angel cake pan

On to utensils. There always seem to be too many in your drawer until you have a party, and then there are never enough. So what do you need? Well, that depends on who you are and what you're going to be doing. There are thousands of utensils, and if you have them all, that's great; but the bare essentials are what I want you to have first (then you can go nuts on your own).

Unlike pots and pans, utensils don't have to be the fanciest ones out there. Some of my favorite wooden spoons I've picked up in the Dollar Store. You will need the following: at least three wooden spoons, a peeler, a spatula, a cheese grater, a can opener, a bottle opener, a corkscrew, a strainer, a colander, a wooden fork, a metal fork, a slotted metal spoon, a whisk, a rubber spatula, a soup ladle, a gravy ladle, a 4-cup measuring cup, a set of measuring spoons, a pastry brush, an ice cream scoop, a meat thermometer, an 8-inch pie plate, a rolling pin, and at least three sizes of mixing bowls. Seems like a lot, but it's just the bare essentials. Obviously, if you're planning to do a lot of entertaining, you need to pick up extra serving spoons.

Electrical appliances are always a plus but not essential. They have made my career as a chef a heck of a lot easier. I recommend obtaining, at some point, a blender, a can opener, a Cuisinart food processor, a hand beater, and a heavy-duty mixer. There are a ton more out there; I treat myself to a new appliance every year to expand my creativity and curiosity. There seems to be an appliance for just about anything you want to do.

Kitchen sanitation is a healthy way to make sure you're eating uncontaminated foods. It's practiced simply by keeping yourself, your utensils, and your area clean. You can always tell the professionals

Substituting Equipment

Remember when I said that you don't have to own every piece of kitchen equipment to cook well? Here are some possible substitutes.

If you don't have	*you could use*
Cookie cutter	A lightly floured glass
Funnel	Snip the corner off a plastic bag for a disposable funnel.
Pie weights	Dried beans (may be reused over and over)
Rotary egg beater	A wire whisk
Rolling pin	An empty wine bottle
Sifter	A sieve or strainer and a wooden spoon
Strawberry huller	Beer can opener or a hard plastic drinking straw
Double boiler	Many professionals cook in a small heavy pot or a heatproof bowl placed in a skillet or other heavy pan filled with $1/2$ inch of water. Thus, the food is cooked evenly all around. Also, it's easy to tell when to lower the heat, add more water, or even remove the pan briefly from the heat.
Heavy pan	Place a thin pan on a skillet for stovetop cooking or on a baking sheet for oven cooking.
Heavy baking sheet	Stack two baking sheets together.
Slow cooker	Place the food in a baking dish. Bake at 200 degrees for 8 to 10 hours.
Steamer	Place a wire rack in a Dutch oven or large saucepan approximately 2 inches off the bottom of the pan. Place the food in a heatproof bowl on the wire rack. Cover tightly and steam.
Tight pan lid	Cover the top of the pan with foil or a double thickness of waxed paper; add the pan lid and press down tightly.

A Few Basic Cooking Terms

Term	Definition
Cube:	To cut a food into pieces 1/2 inch or larger on each side. Use a chef's knife to make lengthwise cuts of the desired width; then cut crosswise to make cubes.
Dice:	To cut a food into cubes 1/8 to 1/4 inch in size. Use a chef's knife to cut into strips of the desired width. Pile the strips together, and cut crosswise into cubes.
Chop:	To cut a food into irregular pea-sized pieces. Use a chopper, blender, food processor, or chef's knife.
Mince:	To cut a food into very tiny irregular pieces. Use a utility knife. Mincing is primarily used for garlic.
Shred:	To cut or shave a food into long, narrow strips, usually by rubbing it across a shredding surface. Use a shredder for most vegetables and for cheeses.
Finely shred:	To rub a food across a fine shredding surface to form very narrow strips. Use when tiny pieces of potent seasonings are needed.
Grate:	To rub a food against a rough perforated utensil to produce slivers, chunks, curls, etc. Grate potent seasonings such as gingerroot, and hard cheeses such as Parmesan.

because they clean as they go—washing hands, cutting boards, utensils, and equipment every time they finish with one food and/or procedure. By this I mean that if you're cutting chicken, and then want to chop lettuce in the same place, you must clean the knife, the cutting board, and your hands before preparing the lettuce. This ensures that no harmful bacteria get transmitted from the chicken to your hands, to the knife, to the board, to the lettuce, and ultimately to you. Here are some tools for kitchen cleanliness: aluminum foil, Saran Wrap, paper towels, plastic food bags, freezer storage bags, waxed paper, Scotch cleaning pads, SOS pads, and some good ole detergent.

Lastly, there are herbs and spices I think you just can't live without. Now that you have the tools, utensils, pots, and pans, you need flavors. Herbs are the aromatic leaves of herbaceous plants (plants that have soft stems rather than bark stems). Herbs are used as an enhancement of flavor and also as a main ingredient, like dill in a dill Hollandaise. Spices, on the other hand, come from the seeds, bark, fruit or flower of the plant. They are used to add flavor and/or color to many dishes.

I have a collection of spices and herbs that I swear by: basil, oregano, red pepper flakes, cinnamon, dillweed, paprika, rosemary, black pepper, allspice, cloves, and parsley. Also, there is an abundance of pre-mixed packaged spices you can buy, like the good old Italian herb mix (which I use in everything), products put out by Goya and Lawry's, and many more. Find one you like and stick with it; there are lots of good products out there for you to stumble upon. Don't become discouraged—if you don't find one you like the first time, give that one to your mother-in-law and go get yourself another one. Soon you may find one or two or three of them you really like. And use them—remember, there is no one telling you that you can't. You make the rules—if you like it, do it.

Along with all these things, I'd like to stress that you don't have to have everything and you don't have to make everything from scratch. There are some wonderful products out there to use as a base for something great. I've always been a fan of pre-made tomato sauce, because I never have time to make it from scratch. Instead of feeling like I'm cheating, I doctor up the jar of sauce. There are no tomato sauces out there that are perfect by themselves, but add some garlic, onions, basil, red pepper flakes, and ground beef, and you've got a new creation—so close to homemade, why should you fuss with the time to make it from scratch when this way is almost as good and much simpler. I'm not saying homemade isn't better, but this way, with improvisations, is pretty darn close. So if you have the time to make it from scratch and know how to do it, more power to you, but it's not mandatory to do so to be a good cook.

One of my favorite things to do is watch a cooking show where the chef makes a pie crust from scratch and passes the recipe on to you. Well, ladies and gentlemen, hold on to your hats: If you haven't tried Pillsbury pre-made pie crusts (found in the refrigeration section of the grocery), you're doing yourself a big disservice. If you can make a better one, it's a fine wonder! It's not cheating to make your life easier. There are hundreds of such products; the trick is to find one that's pretty good and make it better (or simply make life easier for you). This is going to take practice, too. You're not just going to buy a jar of sauce and have it work; you need to mix and match to find some ingredients that make it better. Practice makes perfect, whether you're sprucing up a pre-made ingredient or doing it from scratch.

Just remember that you don't have to be Betty Crocker to be a good cook—you just have to be daring enough to try new things.

Cooking Technique Keys

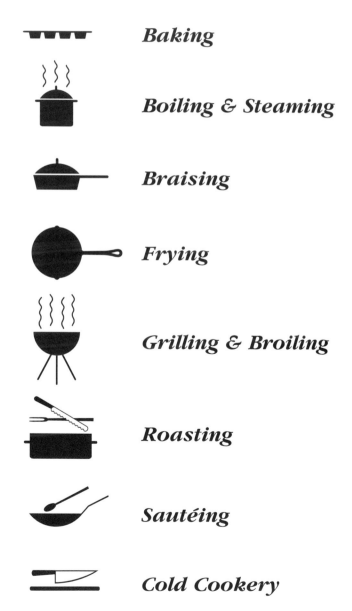

Baking

Boiling & Steaming

Braising

Frying

Grilling & Broiling

Roasting

Sautéing

Cold Cookery

Baking

One of my dearest memories as a child was my grandmother in the kitchen, baking away. She probably never categorized cooking by techniques, as I have done, but I know this was her particular favorite. I think everyone can relate to the smell of cookies baking in the oven. The aroma permeates the rooms and sends your taste buds soaring and your mouth watering in anticipation of those cookies being done. Forget waiting for them to cool—grab a glass of milk and chow them hot! The simple satisfaction that first bite gives you, the warm feelings invoked, are the memories made with that simple baked product. Hopefully, there's a memory like that for you, and think how many memories you can create like that for someone you love.

The technique of baking has many facets to it. Baking can be one of the simplest forms of cooking and simultaneously one of the most difficult. It takes many shapes, sizes, and forms, but one thing stays the same: It is done in some sort of oven.

When we think of baking, it usually turns our thoughts to those cookies and cakes. Baking has many forms, however, as simple as a casserole or as complex as a soufflé. When baking, it is essential to have proper measurements, temperatures, and bakeware. You must know the rules and follow them. This will ensure that you become a more successful baker. This is where the science of ingredients comes into play to produce perfection. Many ingredients like yeasts, baking powder, and baking soda, which are also referred to as leaveners, need precise measurements and temperatures.

Bakeware is the term for a wide variety of utensils used for baking foods in the oven. They're usually made of metal, glass, or ceramic. It's important to know which bakeware is used for what types of foods, so that you may properly cook the dishes you want to bake. If you have all of the following, that's great, but they all take up space, so get what you need for your preferred type of cooking. Remember, it's not how much you have, but having what you need that's important.

When selecting metal bakeware, choose the heaviest ones of a quality you can afford, because they will last the longest and produce the best results. Aluminum pans are a great heat conductor for even heating but cannot be used with dishes that contain acids (tomatoes, marinades, citrus) because there will be a reaction that will ruin the pan and the flavor of the food. Stainless steel is a poor conductor of heat, but it's the easiest of them all to clean. Not only the material composition of the pan, but its exterior and interior are important as well. Pans that have dark and/or dull surfaces absorb heat quicker, reduce cooking times, and make for a crisp crust. On the other hand, shiny or light-colored surfaces are best for cakes because they produce a lighter, more delicate crust. Nonstick interiors of course make for an easy cleanup; but pans that are not cleansed properly will result in a poor non-sticking effect. Finally, pans made out of glass and ceramic tend to hold the heat better, but they heat slower; they also have no reaction with foods.

Timely Tip

Because they tend to hold heat better, when using glass and/or dark bakeware, reduce the oven temperature by 25 degrees to prevent overcooking.

Again, if you have all these types of bakeware, that's great. If not, get what you need. Hopefully, the following descriptions will help you make your decisions.

Baking dishes are open pans that are round, rectangular, or square in shape, are made of glass or ceramic; and come in all different sizes. They are best suited for casseroles that need long exposure times to heat. They are also ideal for freezer and refrigerator storage.

Baking pans, also referred to as cake pans, are square or rectangular, with 1½-inch-high sides. They're usually used for cake and cookie batters but can also be used for roasting.

Baking sheets, commonly known as cookie sheets, are flat metal sheets with a lip on one or more sides, used for cooking stiff doughs for cookies, biscuits, and rolls.

A *bundt pan* is a fluted tubular-shaped pan used for bundt cakes.

A *baking stone* (also known as a pizza stone) is round or square-shaped and made of unglazed stone. Baking stones are used to cook doughs with a light but crisp crust.

A *cake pan,* also known as a layer pan, is 8 or 9 inches round with 1½-inch or higher sides and is used for cakes.

Casserole dishes are made of ceramic or glass and may have a cover.

How to Measure

Measurements are important for consistent results, but not all ingredients are measured in the same way. Learn to measure properly and accurately to guarantee success every time.

To Measure

To measure liquids	use a standard glass or clear plastic measuring cup. Place it on a level surface and bend down so your eye is level with the marking you wish to read. Fill the cup to the desired marking.
	Don't lift the cup off the counter to your eye; your hand won't be as steady or as level as a counter top.
To measure dry ingredients	use a dry measure with exactly the capacity you wish to measure. Pile the ingredient lightly into the cup with a spoon, then level off with a metal spatula.
	Don't pack dry ingredients except for brown sugar, which must be packed into the cup so that it holds the shape of the measure when turned out.
	In years past, it was essential to sift all-purpose flour to lighten it for accurate measurement and to remove any lumps. Today's flour is no longer lumpy and compact; stirring it before measuring is sufficient.

To Measure

To measure flour	stir it in the canister to lighten it. Then gently spoon it into a dry measure, and level off the top with a metal spatula. Cake flour, which is very soft and tends to pack down, and confectioners' sugar should still be sifted.
To measure solid shortening	pack it into a dry measure using a spatula. Run the spatula through the shortening in the cup to make sure there are no air pockets remaining. The easiest way to measure butter or margarine is to use a quarter-pound stick for 1/2 cup, half a stick for 1/4 cup, or one eighth of a stick for 1 tablespoon.
To measure dried herbs	lightly fill a measuring spoon to the top, keeping the level as close to the top as possible. Empty the spoon into your hand and crush the herb with your other hand, or use a mortar and pestle. This breaks the leaves to better release their flavor.
What's a dash?	A dash of an ingredient is actually a measure of less than 1/8 teaspoon (the smallest amount you can accurately measure using standard measuring spoons). When a dash is called for, the ingredient is for seasoning, and the actual amount is up to you. Consider a dash to be about 1/16 teaspoon; taste and adjust amounts if needed.

They are used for slow cooking and are measured by quart sizes. Obviously, they are mostly used for casseroles.

Corn stick pans are made of cast iron, usually with five or six corn-shaped molds. They are used to make corn bread.

Loaf pans, with a standard size of 3x5x9 inches, are used for yeast breads, quick breads, pound cakes, fruitcakes, and meat loaves.

Medallion pans are shell-shaped oval mold pans used to make medallions (similar to cookies).

Muffin pans are rectangular pans with six to twelve cup-shaped cavities that hold muffin or cake batters.

Pie plates are round glass containers used for cooking pies (pie pans are the metal version of these).

Pizza pans are round pans with raised rims for cooking pizzas.

Springform pans are round, two-piece baking pans with removable siding. They come in a variety of diameters.

Tart pans have a shallow fluted side, often removable, in various shapes. They are used to make tarts.

Tube pans are rounded baking pans with a hollow tube center that is used to conduct heat to the center of what you're cooking (typically cakes). Some may even have removable bottoms.

There are dozens of pans to use in the oven but those listed above are the major players in the game of baking. Some are self-explanatory because of their names, like tart pans for tarts, but can also be used for all sorts of cooking. Again, the more you experiment, the better you will become at interchanging your tools while cooking.

Baking has become one of the most versatile cooking techniques. Its uses and creations are limitless. Think of all the wonderful dishes done with baking: the slow process of baking beans for two days, baking breads, having a leftover as a casserole, baking lasagna, apple pies, meat loaves, a baked ham—the list is endless.

But with baking comes the need for precision and exactness in measurements, temperature, and time. Especially when it comes to baking desserts and breads, it is imperative that you use exact measurements of flour, sugar, eggs, and leaveners because in this type of cooking there is chemistry involved between the ingredients, the time, and the temperature. So while baking is one of the oldest techniques, it is also one of the most complex and scientific of them all.

In baking, you must first mix the ingredients exactly as specified in the recipe.

Secondly, you need to select what you're going to use for bakeware. The pan type will usually be specified if it is important to the recipe's completion.

This is just as important as the other steps: You must preheat the oven to the proper temperature. Then, cook as directed, for the time allotted or otherwise specified.

This may be the least forgiving of all the techniques, but it is certainly one of the most rewarding. Baking can be difficult to master, but it is educational and fun to learn.

Baking Template

1. Preheat the oven.
2. Mix the ingredients.
3. Select a baking dish to use and butter the dish if necessary.
4. Bake at the proper temperature and for the time directed.
5. Allow to cool when done.
6. Serve.

Rhubarb Crisp

serves 5

Topping:
1/2 cup butter, softened
1/2 cup packed brown sugar
1/2 cup flour
2 tablespoons ground cinnamon

Rhubarb Filling:
5 cups diced rhubarb (bite-size pieces)
1/2 cup sugar
1/2 cup flour

Mix the topping ingredients together until crumbly. Mix the filling ingredients together. Pour the filling into a buttered casserole dish. Top with the topping. Bake in a preheated 350-degree oven for 45 minutes; cover with foil if the top begins to brown too much. Let cool for 10 minutes before serving.

Variation

• Variations are as simple as using a different fruit, such as strawberries, blueberries, or raspberries, or a combination of fruits.

Boiling & Steaming

Almost everyone has cooked pasta, simmered a soup, or poached an egg. Yet the chances are good that you may never have considered that all these foods were cooked by a technique that we call boiling. Whether this technique is used alone or combined with others to produce a final product, it is sure to be part of many recipes. For instance, we must melt the chocolate before we dip the strawberries, we need a simmering stock before we can make a stew, we must simmer the gravy to make it thicker or more flavorful, we need boiling water to make tea, and we need hard-cooked eggs to make the potato salad—the list goes on and on.

Boiling is the action of liquid at different temperatures used to cook food. When we bring something to a boil, we heat the liquid until bubbles break the surface. Boiling happens to liquids when they reach a temperature of 212 degrees Fahrenheit or 100 degrees Celsius, and for every 1,000 feet above sea level, the boiling point decreases by 2 degrees Fahrenheit. Should you wish to check the different stages, simply put a half-full pot of water on the stove and turn it on high. Notice the bubbles begin small on the bottom and then surface in much larger bubbles as the water's temperature rises. When the bubbles surge and rise faster and faster toward the top, the water has reached the boiling point.

Now turn the burner on a lower heat and watch the rolling boil begin to fall back into the pot. When the violent tossing of water has begun to have a more controlled bubbling motion from the bottom of the pan rather than the top, this is what we refer to as simmering (the most gentle form of boiling). Simmering may also be referred to as poaching. When we poach, we cook a food in simmering liquid. Simmering or poaching denotes faint but slowly bubbling liquid that hardly ever disturbs the top of the liquid. For example, you may want to simmer a stew to vaporize some of the liquid to enhance the flavor of the stew.

Poaching Tips

When poaching eggs, add a small amount of vinegar to the water to help the egg maintain its shape.

Poaching fruit in sugar or wine syrup helps it retain its shape and imparts flavor to the fruit as well.

Begin poaching fish or poultry in a cold liquid, such as a broth or stock, to ensure even cooking and to prevent the fish from flaking apart.

When cooking rice, always add the rice to a rapidly boiling liquid. This will keep the rice from sticking together.

Blanching is yet another form of boiling. Blanching means cooking foods, usually vegetables, briefly in boiling water and then quickly cooling them in cold water. Foods are blanched for one or more of these reasons: to loosen or remove skin (like on peaches, tomatoes, almonds), to enhance color and reduce bitterness

Boiling Vegetables

Vegetable	Minutes	Suggested Seasonings
Artichokes	10 to 15	Dill, French dressing, lemon butter
Asparagus spears tips, pieces	 10 to 20 5 to 15	Mustard seeds, sesame seeds, tarragon, lemon butter, nutmeg, dry mustard, caraway seeds
Beans, lima	25 to 30	Savory, tarragon, thyme, marjoram, oregano, sage
Beans, snap	12 to 16	Basil, dill, marjoram, mint, mustard seeds, oregano, savory, tarragon, thyme
Beets young, whole older, whole sliced	 30 to 45 45 to 90 15 to 25	Allspice, bay leaves, caraway seeds, cloves, dill, ginger, mustard seeds, savory, thyme, orange, celery seeds, nutmeg, vinegar
Broccoli	10 to 15	Seasoned butters, dill, caraway seeds, mustard seeds, tarragon
Brussels sprouts	15 to 20	Basil, caraway seeds, dill, mustard seeds, sage, thyme, lemon butter
Cabbage shredded wedges	 3 to 10 10 to 15	Caraway seeds, celery seeds, dill, mint, mustard seeds, nutmeg, savory, tarragon, peppers
Carrots young, whole older, whole sliced	 15 to 20 20 to 30 10 to 15	Allspice, bay leaves, caraway seeds, dill, fennel, ginger, mace, marjoram, mint, nutmeg, thyme, cloves, curry powder, parsley flakes
Cauliflower flowerets whole	 8 to 15 15 to 25	Caraway seeds, celery salt, dill, mace, tarragon, seasoned butters, sesame seeds, poppy seeds

Vegetable	Minutes	Suggested Seasonings
Celery	15 to 18	Seasoned butters
Corn on the cob	5 to 15	Green pepper, paprika, garlic powder, onion salt
Eggplant	8 to 15	Marjoram, oregano, dill
Greens	10 to 30	Pan drippings from meats, peppers, onion
Okra	10 to 15	Pan drippings from meats
Onions	15 to 30	Caraway seeds, mustard seeds, nutmeg, oregano, sage, thyme
Parsnips whole quartered	20 to 40 8 to 15	Parsley, onion, dill, lemon butter
Peas	12 to 16	Basil, dill, marjoram, mint, oregano, poppy seeds, rosemary, sage, savory
Potatoes whole, medium quartered diced	25 to 40 20 to 25 10 to 15	Basil, bay leaves, caraway seeds, celery seeds, dill, chives, mustard seeds, oregano, poppy seeds, thyme
Spinach	3 to 10	Basil, mace, marjoram, nutmeg, oregano, vinegar
Squash summer, sliced winter, chopped	8 to 15 15 to 20	Allspice, basil, cinnamon, cloves, fennel, ginger, mustard seeds, nutmeg, rosemary, garlic
Sweet potatoes	30 to 55	Allspice, cardamom, cinnamon, cloves, nutmeg
Tomatoes, chopped	7 to 15	Basil, bay leaves, celery seeds, oregano, sage, sesame seeds, tarragon, thyme
Turnips and rutabagas whole chopped	20 to 30 10 to 20	Cloves, ginger, onion, caraway seeds

(good for raw vegetables to be served with dips), and to extend the storage life of raw vegetables to be frozen.

There is yet another form of boiling referred to as steeping, which means to extract flavor from a spice, herb, or root. A familiar example of steeping occurs with tea. In order to make tea, we must steep the herbs and roots.

You may also hear of the term "to steam"—this, too, is a process done by boiling. This type of boiling can be done with a steamer, which usually has a wire basket that sits just over the liquid, but not in it. When boiling, the food will reduce the temperature of the boiling water in which you have immersed it, but in steaming, the food never enters the water, so the temperature remains the same. Therefore, the steam evaporate is actually hotter than the water itself. Many people prefer steaming because steaming seals in flavors, a steamed food doesn't break down as easily since it is not sitting in the water, and steamed foods are less caloric because nothing is added. The most popular steamed items are vegetables.

A recurring theme throughout this book is that most of these cooking techniques can be and are combined with others to make the final dish, but it is important to remember that each technique can stand on its own as well.

Another important aspect of this book I hope you will pick up on is that it doesn't matter what the technique is, usually you can cook just about any food with it. This technique is no different. You may choose chicken, beef, lamb, pork, vegetables, fish, or crustaceans (lobster, clams, crabs, shrimp, etc.) as the food to cook.

Let's recap the boiling technique. First, choose a pot, making sure it is big

Steaming Seafood

Seafood	Minutes
Clams	5 to 10
Crab	5 to 10
Crayfish	5 to 8
Lobster	5 to 10
Mussels	4 to 8
Oysters	8 to 10
Shrimp	3 to 5

Steaming Vegetables

Vegetables	Minutes
Artichokes	25 to 35
Asparagus spears	8 to 12
tips, pieces	5 to 8
Beans (lima)	10 to 15
Beans (snap)	10 to 15
Broccoli	15 to 20
Brussels sprouts	15 to 25
Cabbage	9 to 14

Vegetables	Minutes
Carrots	
young, whole	8 to 12
older, whole	12 to 20
sliced	5 to 10
Cauliflower	
flowerets	10 to 18
whole	20 to 25
Celery	10 to 14
Corn on the cob	8 to 10
Eggplant	4 to 5
Okra	15 to 20
Onions	20 to 25
Parsnips	
whole	15 to 25
quartered	7 to 15
Peas	3 to 12
Potatoes	
whole, medium	30 to 40
diced	8 to 10
Spinach	15 to 20
Squash,	
summer, sliced	4 to 7
winter, chopped	9 to 12
Sweet potatoes	30 to 40
Turnips and rutabagas	
whole	25 to 45
chopped	7 to 12

enough to cook the food. Put enough water in the pot to immerse the food, or just enough water in the bottom to produce a steam.

Then, you need to decide which type of boiling to do, whether it be steaming, poaching, simmering, boiling, or steeping. Try each one; the type you choose determines the time it will take to cook.

Then, you need to pick a liquid to use. The most widely used boiling liquid is water. If you want to add a little flavor, mix in a little wine, stock, and/or marinade. There is no right or wrong in how much you use or blend with others. Remember, you are the chef and it's your taste that will guide you. As with most everything we do, trial and error determines what you do or don't like. That's what makes cooking so much fun. You can boil the same food—take chicken, for example—but if the liquid or herbs you use are different each time, you will have a very differently flavored chicken each time. Same technique, but very different flavors.

Lastly, you may choose to add herbs or spices. Anytime herbs or spices are added to a boiling liquid, the process of steeping will take place. Check the charts at the back of this book (pages 198 through 202) and try adding some herbs and spices to the chosen liquid. This simple act will lead you to a whole different flavor in the food you are cooking.

What are you waiting for? Start boiling!

Boiling Template

1. Prepare the ingredients (chop, peel, measure, etc.).
2. Choose the liquid to cover the food to be cooked.
3. Decide whether to simmer or boil.
4. Cook for the necessary length of time.

Beef Stroganoff

serves 4

¹/₄ cup butter
1¹/₂ pounds cubed beef chuck
¹/₂ cup diced onion
3 cups quartered mushrooms
¹/₄ cup flour
4 cups (about) beef stock (enough
    to cover all ingredients)

1 tablespoon oregano
1 tablespoon basil
1 teaspoon pepper
¹/₄ cup sour cream

Melt the butter in a sauté pan. Sauté the beef, onion and mushrooms in the butter for 5 minutes. Dust with the flour. Place the beef mixture in a stockpot. Cover with beef stock. Add the oregano, basil and pepper and mix well. Simmer over medium heat for 1 hour, stirring frequently. Stir in the sour cream just before serving. Serve over rice or egg noodles.

Braising

What is braising? It's a cooking technique used to tenderize tough cuts of meat and fibrous vegetables. When we hear people say they're going to make a pot roast, or they're going to simmer something in beer, or even that they're going to stew something, what all of these are describing is braising.

Braising consists of many different steps and methods. Let's say you are going to braise a piece of meat—first you must sear the meat. Searing is a method used to expose the food (meat in this case) to a very high heat. Searing quickly browns the outside (forming a crust around the food) while sealing in the juices. Before searing, you may want to season the meat with herbs and spices and you may even roll it in flour before it hits the frying pan.

Timely Tip

Rolling meat in flour and then searing it in the frying pan will make a nice browned base for a gravy once the liquid is added.

Searing can be done in a skillet or a sauté pan (a.k.a. frying pan) with a little oil or butter (just enough to coat the bottom of the pan); or searing can be done in the oven on broil in a short-sided pan, just long enough to brown the food; it can also be done on the grill by slowly rolling the food as it browns to form an even coat.

The first step to braising on the grill is searing the food by charcoal roasting.

Then, you can add the liquid to the food. The type of liquid used can be just about anything, although the differences in flavor from one to another can vary greatly. Water is definitely the first liquid to come to mind, but it will need additional seasoning and even some vegetables. A simple stock of some sort—beef, chicken, or vegetable stock (better known as broth)—will enhance the flavor of your food. You can also use cider, wine, beer, juices, and/or marinades: each will have its own special end result. It's perfectly all right to combine the liquids.

Once the food is seared, place it in a pan not much bigger than the food itself; add the liquid, about halfway covering the food, and make sure you have a lid to cover it all. The liquid within the pot will begin to produce aromatic vapors (steam) that will be trapped by the lid and forced back into the meat, providing a long, moist, tenderizing treatment. This will produce tender, flavorful meat.

You may find this similar to boiling or poaching; the main difference is that the food is seared. Otherwise, the method is primarily the same. You may wish to get fancy and throw in some vegetables with the food being braised. Some fibrous vegetables to include are carrots, onions, celery, turnips, potatoes, leeks, and parsnips. You can add the vegetables in as a bed for the seared food to sit on. Now add your liquid and begin cooking.

Cooking can be done in the oven at 350 degrees, or on the stove over medium-high heat. Don't limit yourself only to meat—try chicken, fish, sweetbreads, and vegetables. The liquid supplies the necessary moisture because the cooking is done mainly by the flavored steam, as opposed to a simmering liquid.

Let's recap our procedures. First, you must pick a food or a combination of foods. The choices can include a cut of beef, pork, or lamb; a whole chicken; veal shanks; a whole fish or a fillet of a large fish; and those fibrous vegetables such as carrots, turnips, onions, and potatoes. (When picking a cut of meat, I usually try to pick out tougher cuts since braising will tenderize the food. Try shanks, top rounds, bottom rounds, or whole legs.)

Once you have chosen a food to cook, then you can choose a liquid or a combination of liquids. Liquids can include water, wine, beer, beef stock, chicken stock, store-bought or homemade marinades, pineapple juice, tomato juice, or orange juice. Once you have picked the food and the liquid, you're about ready to begin.

To start, you must first sear the food, which seals in the juices. Then add enough liquid to reach halfway up the food, which will keep the food from drying out and will also keep it tender. Now you're ready to begin cooking.

Timely Tip

When picking a liquid, I always have a base of water or stock and then add another flavor of liquid in a ratio of 2 to 1 (2 parts stock or water and 1 part marinade, for example).

Now that you know the technique, go out and buy yourself something to braise and try lots of combinations. You're bound to like the end result with dozens.

Braising Times

Food	*Time*
Beef	
Arm pot roast	2 to 3 hours
Blade roast	2 to 3 hours
Rump roast	3 to 4 hours
Round steak, 1 inch	1 to 1½ hours
Flank steak	1½ hours
Round steak	2 to 3 hours
Short ribs	1½ to 2½ hours
Chicken	
3 pounds	35 to 50 minutes
5 pounds	2 hours
Stews	1½ to 2 hours
Fish	
All Types	10 minutes per inch of thickness
Lamb	
Breast, stuffed	1½ to 2 hours
Breast, not stuffed	1½ to 2 hours
Chops	35 to 40 minutes
Neck slices	1 to 1¼ hours
Riblets	1½ to 2 hours
Shanks	1½ to 2 hours
Rolled shoulder	2 to 2½ hours
Stews	1½ to 2 hours
Pork	
Back ribs	1½ to 2 hours
Spareribs	1½ hours
Loin chops	35 to 60 minutes
Rib chops	35 to 60 minutes
Cubed	45 to 60 minutes
Shoulder steaks	45 to 60 minutes
Tenderloin, whole	45 to 60 minutes
Tenderloin, fillets	30 minutes
Ham	25 to 30 minutes per pound

Food	Time
Turkey	
Drumsticks	1¹/₂ hours
Thighs	2 hours
Wings	1¹/₂ hours
Wing drumettes	2 hours
Veal	
Rolled shoulder	2 to 2¹/₂ hours

Braising Template

1. Sear the main food.
2. Add the other ingredients.
3. Add seasoning.
4. Add enough liquid to reach ³/₄ of the way up the other ingredients.
5. Bake in a preheated oven or cover and simmer on the stove.
6. Serve.

Braised Chicken Thighs

2 tablespoons olive oil
2 pounds chicken thighs
  (leave skin on and bone in)
2 cups coarsely diced onions
¹/₄ cup coarsely diced yellow or
  orange peppers
¹/₂ cup quartered mushrooms
1 tablespoon minced garlic
1 teaspoon thyme
1 can cream of chicken soup
1¹/₂ soup cans water

serves 4

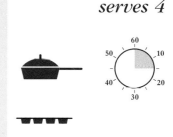

Heat the olive oil in a sauté pan over high heat. Add the chicken skin side down. Sear for 5 minutes or until the skin is crisp. Remove the chicken to a plate. Combine the onions, peppers, mushrooms, garlic and thyme in the sauté pan. Sauté for 2 minutes. Place the vegetable mixture in a deep casserole dish. Place the chicken skin side down over the vegetables. Mix the soup with the water and pour enough into the casserole dish to reach ³/₄ of the way up the vegetable mixture. Bake in a preheated 350-degree oven for 1 hour, turning the chicken once. (You may instead cook this dish in a braising pot on the stovetop. Cover and simmer for about 45 minutes.) If you wish, strain out the liquid and bring it to a boil to thicken for a gravy.

Frying

Frying is both the fastest and the most widely understood of all the techniques. To fry means to immerse a food entirely in hot fat so that the exterior of the food is quickly seared (crisp and brown) around a moist, perfectly cooked interior.

The first prerequisite of frying is to select a fryer. You will find that there is a plethora of choices for you out there. Some of these include electric deep fryers with thermostatic controls, Dutch ovens, electric skillets, and the good old traditional wide pans designed for frying. Some may even have a basket that fits into the pan and can be hooked to the side of the bar to drain. Note that if you are using a non-electric pan you'll have to get a deep frying thermometer to gauge the temperature properly. Also, if you don't have a basket, you'll need something to scoop out the food being fried, such as a slotted spoon, wire skimmer, or tongs (to lift out larger pieces).

Frying has received an undeserved bad reputation throughout the years. People are becoming more concerned with caloric intake and the amount of fat in their diets. It's a basic misconception that frying is directly linked to greasy foods high in fat. What most don't know is that when the frying technique is done correctly at the proper temperatures, fried foods will absorb only a minimum of fat.

The proper way to fry foods is to begin with a good oil. All kinds of fats (oils) can be used. Today the most widely used oils are vegetable, corn, peanut, and soybean. Sometimes other fats such as lard and solid shortenings are used. The best fats for frying have a high smoke point, which is the temperature at which the fat smokes and begins to break down. (Fat should never be allowed to smoke. Smoking is a sign that the oil is beginning to break down and this will both ruin the flavor of the foods and fry them unevenly.) Good oil choices are corn, peanut, and safflower. These oils can be used over and over again as long as the oil is drained and strained after each use. Never use oil that is too dark to see through, smokes when heated, or has a funky odor.

Fill your fryer with oil and be generous about it (although you want to leave enough space at the top of the fryer to allow room for the food). Make sure you have enough fat to entirely cover the food being fried. When frying, never overcrowd the pan; you want to allow all of the oil to circulate around the food. Frying in small batches will also make a crisper, less greasy food.

The single most important factor in frying is proper temperature. Much of the negative perception of frying is due to improper cooking temperatures and to overcrowding the pan. These conditions make for a soggy, greasy, limp outside and a hard inside (mostly, lots of absorbed fat). After each small batch of frying, you should allow the fat to reheat to the proper temperature before adding the next batch of food to be fried. If possible, always regulate the temperature with a deep fat thermometer.

Timely Tip

If you don't have a thermometer, you can test the temperature with a cube of white bread. Throw the cube of bread into the hot fat; if the bread browns in one minute, the temperature is approximately 350 degrees Fahrenheit (40 seconds, approximately 365 to 380 degrees; 20 seconds, approximately 380 to 390 degrees; and so on).

Once the fat reaches the correct temperature, you are ready to begin frying. Many things are fried in their natural shell, such as potatoes and plantain bananas. Some things are dusted with flour to produce a golden brown coating (the best example being fried chicken). Others are coated with a batter to insulate the delicate food with a light, crisp, puffy coating. (The coating holds the delicate food without ruining it.) Also, many foods are battered to add flavor, such as a beer batter for fish or a Cajun batter for Louisiana-style shrimp. Batters can also protect fruits and vegetables when they are being fried.

We also use breading as a form of insulation for foods. Breading is done by lightly coating a food in flour, then dipping it in an egg wash (a mixture of egg(s) and a small amount of water or milk) and rolling it in bread crumbs. When met with the oil, these coatings quickly develop a crunchy, golden brown shell that seals in the tenderness and moisture of the food.

Once the food is fried, place it on a paper towel to absorb any excess grease. If you have more to fry, set the oven on a low temperature to keep the already fried food warm. Allow the oil to regain its temperature before frying any more food. Then, continue the same process.

Remember these simple rules: Heat the oil to the correct temperature. If needed, coat or batter the food. Fry in small batches to allow the food to be entirely immersed in fat. Drain the excess fat on paper towels when done. Allow the oil to regain its proper temperature before frying more.

To recap our frying technique, you must first pick a food. You can choose just about anything you like (chicken, beef, pork, fruits, vegetables, fish, or crustaceans).

Secondly, you must decide whether to coat the food. If so, will it be flour, a batter, or a crumb coating?

Thirdly, you need to choose a fat, preferably a corn, peanut, safflower or soybean oil. You could choose a shortening, lard, or animal fat instead.

Now, you need to choose a fryer. Some of the choices are an electric fryer, a 4- to 5-quart pot, a Dutch oven, an electric skillet, or a sturdy pan. Make sure the fryer will be able to hold the food and fully immerse it in oil.

It's imperative that you cook the food at the proper temperature. See what the recipe calls for and cook in the suggested amount of time and at the suggested temperature. If your fryer doesn't have

Timely Tip

Don't ever leave hot fat unattended: Oil that is allowed to get too hot will ignite. Should this happen, never throw water on it; water will spread the oil and flames, ultimately creating more danger. To put out the flames, cover the pot to cut off the fire's oxygen. If there is no cover around, baking soda and salt thrown on the flames will extinguish the fire.

a thermostat, you will need to buy a fryer thermometer to regulate the temperature.

Frying is undoubtedly a messy, smelly technique and it needs your constant attention, but it is also the fastest way to cook foods. Following the simple steps provided, your food will be cooked perfectly, with little excess fat. Don't be discouraged if it takes time and a few burned results before you get it right. Once you master the timing and skill, you too will be producing delicious dishes in no time at all.

So go ahead and give it a try. Pull that Fry Daddy out of the closet, and try all the coatings and oils until you find the ones best suited for you. There are so many foods out there that you'll never become bored with this technique.

Frying Template

1. Choose a fryer.
2. Choose a fat for the fryer, usually oil.
3. Preheat the fryer and fat to the directed temperature.
4. Prepare the foods to be cooked.
5. Fry, being careful not to overfill the fryer.
6. Drain on paper towels.
7. Serve.

Cajun Fried Catfish

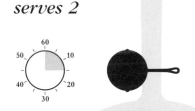

serves 2

1 pound catfish fillets, cut into strips
$1/4$ cup flour
2 eggs, beaten

$1/2$ cup bread crumbs
3 tablespoons Cajun seasoning
$1/2$ teaspoon cayenne
Vegetable oil for frying

Dredge the fish in the flour, discarding any excess flour. Dip the fish into the eggs. Coat the fish with a mixture of the bread crumbs, Cajun seasoning and cayenne. Discard any unused eggs and bread crumbs. Fry the fish a few pieces at a time in 350-degree oil in a skillet for 8 minutes or until the strips float to the top. Drain on paper towels.

Variation

- Use this recipe with most any white flake fish, such as flounder, trout, bass, or grouper.

Grilling & Broiling

Grilling is the technique of cooking a food directly over a heat source—browning the exterior to give it that distinctive grilled flavor but without overcooking the interior. The food can be meat, poultry, seafood, vegetables, fruits, or breads; the heat source can be charcoal, electricity, or gas. Though basically synonymous, in grilling the heat source is below the food and in broiling the heat source is above the food. Then we enter the realm of barbecuing—a long slow grilling process, sometimes done in a pit with large pieces of meat kept moist by that highly seasoned sauce we refer to as barbecue sauce. Barbecuing is generally done at a greater distance from the heat source, and the food is continually brushed with a liquid sauce of sorts (which is referred to as basting). Basting can be done with a marinade (usually a liquid sauce that the food is soaked in), yet marinating and basting can also be one and the same.

Not only is grilling one of the fastest ways to cook, but it cooks out a large amount of fat, and the closeness of the direct heat chars the food's surface to enhance its flavor. The only drawback of grilling that I can see is that it does not tenderize the food being cooked.

It is imperative that the food not be left unattended while being cooked. Attentiveness will help you avoid over-cooking, which leaves the food dried out and burned.

When grilling, you should try to eliminate any extra fat from the food, or any excess oil from a marinade, because the drippings from fat will cause the heat source to flame and char the food.

Timely Tip

When grilling outdoors, keep a spray bottle of water handy. When the flames get out of control, you can spray them with the water to control the cooking. Be careful: excess spraying could lower the heat too much, so be sure to use in moderation.

When grilling, broiling, or barbecuing, make sure you have the proper equipment. Basting brushes, tongs, and forks are all helpful utensils. Try to choose those with handles long enough to let you get closer to the heat without burning your hands. Avoid piercing the food with forks because that allows the juices to escape and will dry out what you are cooking. Never set the utensils on the grill because they may melt, catch fire, or burn you when you go to grab them. Hinged wire baskets in all shapes are particularly helpful in cooking fish, which has a tendency to fall apart. These are also great for small foods that can't be skewered and for vegetables, which tend to be of a more delicate texture. Wooden skewers and metal skewers are helpful for combining vegetables and meats or poultry. Remember when using wooden skewers to allow them to soak in water for thirty minutes so that they will not burn while cooking.

Grilling Meat, Poultry and Seafood

Food	Coals	Minutes
Chicken		
1/2 broiler	Medium	45
Breasts, boneless, skinless	Medium hot	12
Breasts, bone in, with skin	Medium	15 to 20
Thighs and drumsticks	Medium	40
Strips on skewers	Medium hot	8
Turkey		
Breast steak	Medium	14
Drumstick	Medium	50
Thigh	Medium	55
Ground, patties	Medium hot	16
Other Poultry		
1/2 Cornish game hen	Medium hot	45
Fish		
Fillets or steaks, 1-inch	Medium hot	10
Whole	Medium hot	8 minutes per pound
Shellfish		
Clams and mussels	Medium hot	3
Oysters	Medium hot	3
Lobster,		
Split into halves	Medium hot	12
Tails	Medium hot	8 to 12
Sea scallops, on skewers	Medium hot	6
Shrimp on skewers	Medium hot	7 to 10

Food	Coals	Minutes		
Beef		(Rare)	(Med)	(Well)
Tender steaks, 1-inch	Medium hot	10	12	18
Less tender steaks, 1-inch	Medium	14	18	22
Flank steak				
(Not tender if cooked past medium)	Hot		12	
Ground patties				
(Must be cooked well done)	Medium hot			16
Lamb				
Chops	Medium	12	14	
Cubes	Medium hot	12	14	
Pork		(Med Well)		
Chops				
3/4-inch	Medium hot	14		
Steaks				
3/4-inch	Medium hot	14		
Spareribs	Very low	60		
Canadian bacon, 1-inch	Medium	35		
Ham, 1-inch slices	Medium hot	22		
		(Well Done)		
Fresh sausages	Medium hot	12		
Frankfurters	Medium hot	4		
Veal		(Med Well)		
Steak, 1-inch	Medium	20		
Chops, 1-inch	Medium	20		

Grilling Vegetables

Food	Preparation	Coals	Minutes
Asparagus	Trim tough bases of stems; precook for 3 to 4 minutes.	Medium hot	3 to 5
Beans, lima	Wrap in foil packets.	Medium	20
Beans, snap	Wrap in foil packets.	Medium	20
Carrots, whole, young	Precook for 3 to 5 minutes.	Medium hot	3 to 5
Carrots, sliced	Wrap in foil packets.	Medium	25 to 30
Corn on the cob	Remove husks and silks; wrap in foil packets.	Medium	15 to 20
Eggplant	Split into halves lengthwise or cut into 1-inch slices.	Medium hot	8
Fennel	Precook for 10 minutes; cut into wedges.	Medium hot	8
Onions	Cut into 1/2-inch slices.	Medium hot	9
Peas	Wrap in foil packets.	Medium	20
Potatoes, new	Cut into halves; precook for 10 minutes.	Medium hot	11
Potatoes, russet	Cut into 1/2-inch slices; wrap in foil packets.	Medium hot	12
Squash, summer	Cut into halves lengthwise.	Medium hot	6 to 8 minutes

Heavy-duty foil is useful to shield foods on the grill, to wrap a food being cooked, and to allow an area for pan drippings to accumulate. If you're a beginner, buy yourself a meat thermometer so you can tell when the food is done, thus avoiding overcooking.

When preparing to grill or broil food, make sure that what you are cooking it in is properly preheated. If you're broiling it in an electric oven, let the oven light tell you when it's up to temperature. When broiling in an electric oven, leave the oven door slightly ajar (if the door is closed, the thermostat will turn the broiler off). Gas broilers will always have a consistent flame without the door having to be open. When grilling with electricity or gas, you should always follow the manufacturer's instructions for preheating.

Timely Tip

Testing the heat of charcoal can be pretty easy. Place your hand two inches above the metal grill and count (one one hundred, two one hundred) until the heat makes you pull your hand away. The amount of time indicates the temperature of the charcoal. Common sense will tell you that if you only make it to one or two the grill is very hot, but if you make it to three/four it is medium hot, four/five it is medium, and so on.

If it is extremely hot, rearrange the coals to distribute the heat more evenly, which will take anywhere from twenty to thirty minutes to heat sufficiently—you always want the maximum heat for cooking done in the minimum time.

When using sauces on a food being grilled or broiled, baste during the last half of the cooking time to deter excess charring. To avoid bacterial contamination, cook for an extra three minutes after the application of sauce.

Variations of a dish can be as simple as trying the same food in a grill and then a broiler. Then compare the differences.

Timely Tip

For health reasons, never use the same pan or platter for both the uncooked food and the cooked food.

Now let's recap the technique of grilling and broiling. First, pick a food. You may choose more than one, but you must keep them separate unless you are making kabobs. Some of the choices are beef, pork, and lamb, with some of the more obvious cuts being ribs, chops, flank steaks, tenderloins, loins, steaks, and hamburgers; chicken breasts (with or without the bone), wings, drums, or halves (but not whole chickens); whole fish, fish fillets, or fish steaks, with the best being swordfish, grouper, mahi mahi, tuna, and salmon, because the flesh of these fish tends to hold together better. Flakier fish like sole, cod, trout, or simply fish that is too small to fillet can be grilled whole with the skin on or wrapped and cooked in foil. Don't forget that crustaceans can also be grilled or broiled. Such delicacies as shrimp and scallops can also be cooked this way. So can vegetables, although obviously it would be difficult to grill string beans, simply because they would fall through the spaces in the grill! Something like this could be broiled more easily in a pan in the oven. Just about any vegetable you can think of will work: eggplant, bell

Broiling Times

The following are approximate broiling times and distances for some common foods. Because the times are only approximate, you should begin checking doneness at the earliest time mentioned. Times for beef and lamb are given for rare (140 degrees) and medium (160 degrees). However, ground beef patties should be cooked to at least 160 degrees; if you add eggs, bread crumbs, liquids, or other such ingredients, cook them to 170 degrees. You will achieve better results if you marinate tougher cuts of meat in the refrigerator for 6 to 8 hours before broiling.

Food	Inches from Heat	Minutes
Chicken		
Breasts	6 to 8	10 to 20
Broilers, cut into halves	6 to 12	25 to 35
Fish		
Fillets	3 to 4	5 to 10
Steaks		
Small	3 to 4	8 to 13
Large	6	8 to 13
Pork		
Loin chops		
1-inch	3 to 4	15 to 20
Ham slices		
1-inch	3 to 4	13 to 14
Ham cubes, precooked	4	12
Bacon	3	4 to 5
Link sausage	4	12 to 15
Shellfish		
Soft-shell crabs	3	5 to 8
Lobster, split into halves	5	12 to 15
Oysters	3	5 to 8
Sea scallops	3	3 to 5
Shrimp	3	5 to 9
Turkey		
Breast tenderloins	6 to 8	10

Food	Inches from Heat	Minutes	

Veal

Food	Inches from Heat	Minutes	
Loin chops, 1-inch	3 to 4	15 to 20	

Lamb

Food	Inches from Heat	(Rare)	(Medium)
Shoulder chops			
3/4- to 1-inch	3 to 4	7	14
1 1/2-inch	4 to 5	12	22
Rib or loin chops			
1-inch	3 to 4	7	14
1 1/2-inch	4 to 5	15	22
Sirloin chops, 3/4- to 1-inch	3 to 4	12	22
Cubes, 3/4- to 1-inch	4 to 5	8	15

Beef

Food	Inches from Heat	(Rare)	(Medium)
Chuck shoulder steak, boneless			
1-inch	3 to 4	14	18
Chuck blade steak			
1-inch	2 to 3	11	14
Flank steak	2 to 3	12	14
Rib-eye, porterhouse, and T-bone steaks			
1-inch	3 to 4	10	15
Sirloin steaks, boneless			
1-inch	3 to 4	16	30
Sirloin cubes	3 to 4	9	12
Tenderloin steak			
1-inch	2 to 3	10	15
Top loin steak, boneless			
1-inch	3 to 4	12	17
Top round steak			
1-inch	3 to 4	15	18
Short ribs	2 to 3	10	12
Ground beef patties			(Well Done)
1/2-inch	3 to 4		16

peppers, sweet potatoes, carrots, squash, broccoli, and onions are some of my favorites.

Then there are the additions you may use when you're grilling and broiling. You should first decide whether you want to grill the food plain and add nothing or if you want to add flavors. If you choose flavoring, try one of these: Soak or baste the food in a marinade; sprinkle the food with an herb or herbs; spread a rub (a thicker pasty marinade) on the food; or maybe barbecue sauce is what you want. The choices are endless.

A marinade can be as simple as one bought from the store or it can be one you've made. Some of my favorite marinades include soy sauce and pineapple juice with ginger; olive oil with some herbs and spices and a little orange juice; or a simple mustard and honey. Marinades can even be made from a bottle of your favorite salad dressing. There is no right or wrong way to make a marinade; it is a personal preference and will be better demonstrated later in the book. Using rubs can be as simple as

coating the food's exterior with fresh herbs or a ready-made rub you've bought. Lastly, there are very few people I can think of that don't like barbecue sauce; getting a good flavor is as easy as letting the food soak in the sauce—or just baste with it. There are lots of good barbecue sauces out there, so find one you like. And if you feel more daring, try making your own—you'll be surprised how easy it is.

Now that we've covered the technique, try some of the wonderful variations that are out there waiting for you to explore. Go ahead, try it.

Grilling & Broiling Template

1. Prepare the food to be cooked.
2. Prepare the marinade, rub, or barbecue sauce.
3. Heat the grill or broiler.
4. Season if needed.
5. Grill or broil, basting if directed to do so.
6. Serve.

Cranberry Dijon Shrimp

serves 4

³/₄ cup cranberry jelly
¹/₄ cup Dijon mustard

2 pounds shrimp, peeled, deveined

Mix the jelly and Dijon mustard in a bowl. Add the shrimp. Marinate for several minutes. Drain the shrimp, reserving the marinade. Place the shrimp on a hot grill rack. Grill for 5 minutes or until the shrimp feel firm, turning frequently and basting with the reserved marinade.

Roasting

Roasting is a dry cooking technique used for poultry, large pieces of meat, and vegetables in which all sides of the food receive an even heat circulation. It provides a browned exterior and a moist interior. Roasting vegetables will bring out their natural sweet flavors, and some fibrous vegetables, such as carrots and onions, may be roasted alongside the meats.

The food to be roasted should always be placed on a rack in a shallow roasting pan. The rack can be an adjustable V-shaped rack or as simple as a flat rack like the ones you'll find in a broiler pan. The important thing is to never put the food directly on the bottom of a pan. Always use a pan shallow enough to allow the heat to surround the food. You must elevate the food on some sort of rack within the pan because once the food begins to cook, the fats and juices will drain from it. If the pan juices are in contact with the food, the moisture will prevent the food from cooking evenly on the top and bottom, ultimately producing a soggy bottom.

When done properly on a rack in a shallow pan, food will cook evenly on all sides. However, just because it's not cooked in the juices does not mean not to baste it. Basting brings out a flavor all its own. For basting, make sure you have either a large unslotted spoon or a bubble baster.

One of the most essential tools for roasting is a meat thermometer. A proper meat thermometer shouldn't have rare, medium, and well done as guides; it should have temperature readings of 0 to 220 degrees. This tool is basic because each type and cut of meat may have a different internal temperature for each scale of doneness. Never leave a thermometer in the meat while cooking because they are so delicately made that the high temperature of the oven will ruin them. Instead, they should be used toward the end of the cooking time, inserted into the thickest part of the food but not near the bone (the bone is a heat conductor and will give an improper reading).

Timely Tip

Always remove the food from the oven when the thermometer reads 10 degrees lower than desired because the food has a "carryover" cooking time (approximately 15 minutes). This will increase the food's temperature by 10 degrees. (For example, if I want a roast to be cooked medium well, then I should take it out when it is 10 degrees lower than medium well temperature. The heat of the roast itself will carryover cook it to medium well.) It's also important to let the food fully carryover cook (that is, rest for a good 15 minutes) before you cut into it or serve it.

I tend to always have my fingers in everything I cook, and this should be something that you do as well. I feel each food as it cooks and then I read the thermometer, just so I can compare what it feels like when it's done. The more you test this way, the better you will become at it. This will result in you almost being a better gauge than the thermometer in testing a food's doneness.

When you touch a food, it should feel firm, neither soft nor hard, but still with a little resilience. The more experienced you become, the more confidence you'll acquire in trusting your hands to time food. I usually make notes from previous times I have roasted to help me in the future (for instance, how long a five-pound roast took to cook at 375 degrees). With notes such as this, the next time you cook a five-pound roast you can better judge the time needed to cook it perfectly. Check the helpful chart on page 111 for proper cooking temperatures.

Being the great cook that you are, be proud to carve your finished roast for your guests or family. For proper carving, you'll need a sturdy cutting board, a long serrated knife, and a carving fork. Carving can be a tricky procedure, but if you don't try it, you'll never get the hang of it. Much like cooking, the more you do it, the better you'll get at it. Check the following charts for helpful hints on carving.

When you buy a piece of meat for roasting, it is good to have a fatty top coat on the meat. This will ensure that the meat is flavorful due to the drippings and additional moisture that the fat will produce while roasting. We tend to want to season the meat's fatty top to incorporate even more flavor; the food will determine the seasonings. I like to roast everything with salt, pepper, diced onions, and garlic. But the combinations you can use are endless. You may even choose to use a rub as a seasoning. Regardless of what you choose, keep in mind that just because you cooked the food with fat on it doesn't mean you have to serve it that way. However, remember

Carving

Carving is an art that you can take pride in mastering. The instructions and illustrations that follow show the art of carving beef, pork, ham, lamb, chicken, and turkey. By following these instructions, you can be certain that the slices of meat you place on the table will be as good to look at as they are to eat.

Standing Rib Roast

1. Place the roast on the platter with the largest end down to form a solid base. Insert the fork between the two top ribs. Starting across on the fat side, carve across the grain to the rib bone.

2. Use the tip of the knife to cut along the rib bone to loosen the slice. Be sure to keep close to the bone, to make the largest servings possible.

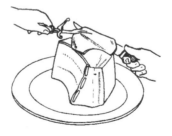

3. Slide the knife back under the slice and, steadying it with the fork, lift the slice to the side of the platter. If the platter is not large enough, place the slices on a heated platter close by.

Chicken and Turkey

1. To remove leg, hold the drumstick firmly with fingers, pulling gently away from the body. At the same time, cut skin between leg and body.

Chicken and Turkey

2. Press leg away from body with flat side of knife. Then cut through joint joining leg to backbone and skin on the back. If the "oyster," a choice oyster-shaped piece lying in the spoon-shaped section of the backbone, was not removed with the thigh, remove it at this point. Separate drumstick and thigh by cutting down through the joint.

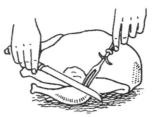

3. Slice drumstick meat. Hold drumstick upright at a convenient angle to plate and cut down, turning drumstick to get uniform slices. Chicken drumsticks and thighs are usually served without slicing.

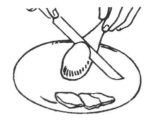

4. Slice thigh meat. Hold thigh tightly on plate with a fork. Cut slices of meat parallel to the bone.

5. Cut into white meat parallel to wing. Make a cut deep into the breast until the knife reaches the body frame, parallel to and as close to the wing as possible.

6. Slice white meat. Beginning at front, starting halfway up the breast, cut thin slices of white meat down to the cut made parallel to the wing. The slices will fall away from the bird as they are cut to this line. Continue carving for first servings. Additional meat may be carved as needed.

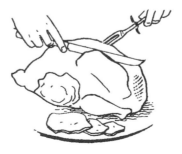

that roasted fat will not only incorporate flavor and moisture, it will also add to the presentation of the final product. Some people, including me, love to pick and eat the roasted crispy fat pieces because they have an abundance of flavor, but let me remind you that you are eating fat—that's what it's loaded with, FAT. So, as with any treat, moderation is best.

So let's recap by going right through the steps for roasting. First, you need to pick out what you're going to roast. Most roasted items are larger tender cuts of meat such as prime rib, steamship round, spareribs, ham, legs of lamb, veal, or pork loin. We also cook a variety of poultry: quartered, half, or whole chickens, turkey (sectioned or whole), and duck. A variety of vegetables are also roasted as a main dish, side dish, and as a prerequisite for another dish. Whole or filleted fish are also roasted to bring flavor to milder fish.

Secondly, you want to season the food as well as trim off the excess fat. You want the food to have a little fat to baste in, but if there is let's say an inch of fat on the meat, then you should trim off a good half inch. You want some fat but not an overabundance of it. You may buy a piece of meat that is already rolled and tied in string; if this is the case, then roast it as is. What it is will determine what you season it with. For beef I recommend garlic, onions, salt, pepper, rosemary, and thyme. Sometimes I omit the rosemary and add mustard and honey for additional flavor. Seasonings for pork can be the same as for beef. With fish, I particularly like roasted red peppers, dill, onions, salt, pepper, and a dash of marjoram. For poultry I like to rub the skin with a little soy sauce, which helps with the browning, and then add salt, pepper, oregano, basil, and a little coriander. With vegetables I will do an assortment of seasonings, but the key to roasting vegetables is to coat them with a little fat (either oil or butter) because they have no fat of their own to roast or brown in. The combinations are endless, and there is no right or wrong in seasonings, so try all sorts—you'll never know what you like unless you try them all. So if someone recommends a seasoning that includes garlic, and you hate garlic, then just omit it, and maybe add something else you like. Or you might decide not to add anything else at all. You are the creator and the chef: if you like a certain combination, give it a try. Maybe you'll be the creator of the block's new favorite seasoning.

Place whatever it is you're roasting on a roasting pan or V rack; then preheat the oven to the proper temperature. If the food you're cooking becomes brown very quickly, pull it out and cover it with foil to prevent if from burning; then continue cooking. While it's cooking, I like to baste it with the drippings that have cooked off about every 15 minutes; this always ensures a flavorful food. Check the internal temperature of the roasting food and take it out 10 degrees under the desired temperature. Let it stand to carryover cook for another 15 minutes before serving and/or cutting. With vegetables and potatoes, you're better off tasting to see if it's cooked to your liking. Both of these should be crisp to the bite yet tender inside. The same advice that applies to vegetables also applies to meat—that is, if the browning takes place then quickly cover loosely with foil and continue cooking until done. Again, check the charts for that desired temperature. When it's done, present it whole or sliced and enjoy.

Roast Leg of Lamb

1. Place the roast on the platter with the shank to the carver's right and the thinnest section on the near side. From this thin section, remove two or three lengthwise slices to form a base.

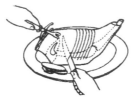

2. Turn the roast up on the base and, starting at the shank end, make slices perpendicular to the leg bone as shown in the illustration.

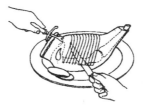

3. After reaching the aitchbone, loosen the slices by cutting under them, following the top of the leg bone. Remove slices to platter and then serve.

Whole Ham

1. Place the ham on a platter with decorated side up and the shank to the carver's right. Remove several slices from the thinnest side to form a solid base on which to set the ham.

2. Turn the ham on its base. Starting at the shank end, cut a small wedge and remove; then carve perpendicular to the leg bone as shown in the illustration.

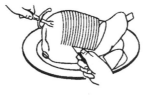

3. Release slices by cutting under them and along the leg bone, starting at the shank end. For additional servings, turn ham over and make slices to the bone; release and serve.

Picnic Shoulder

1. This diagram is your road map for carving attractive servings from a pork picnic shoulder. It may be a baked smoked picnic or a roasted fresh picnic—the method of carving is the same.

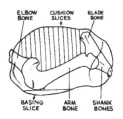

2. Place picnic on platter with fat side up and shank to carver's right. Use fork to anchor picnic, then remove a lengthwise slice from side opposite elbow bone.

3. From the blade bone, cut down to the arm bone. Then turn the knife and cut all along the arm bone. The boneless arm meat will separate from the bones in one piece.

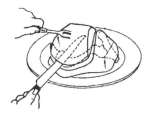

4. Carve boneless arm meat by making perpendicular slices from top side of meat down to platter. It is advisable to carve on a wooden board or a platter with a wooden insert.

Roasting Template

1. Preheat the oven.

2. Season or marinate the food to be cooked.

3. Roast in the oven for the time directed or until the appropriate internal temperature is reached.

4. Remove from the oven. Let cool for 5 minutes before cutting into the food to allow carryover cooking to occur.

5. Garnish and serve.

Lemon Thyme Drumsticks

1 tablespoon lemon peel
2 tablespoons thyme
2 cups pineapple juice

1/4 cup soy sauce
1 1/2 pounds chicken drumsticks

serves 3

Mix the lemon peel, thyme, pineapple juice and soy sauce in a bowl. Add the chicken and marinate for at least 1 hour. Remove the chicken from the marinade and place on a roasting rack. Roast at 375 degrees for 45 minutes. Serve and enjoy.

Roasting and Baking Vegetables

Roasting brings out the natural flavor and sweetness of vegetables. You can roast them alone using the chart below, or you can roast them in the pan with the meat or chicken. Potatoes cooked with a roast should first be parboiled for 5 to 10 minutes; baste occasionally during roasting.

Vegetable	Preparation	Time
Beets	Wrap in foil.	Bake at 375 degrees for 1 to 1¼ hours.
Carrots	Peel and slice. Dot with butter.	Bake, covered, for 40 to 50 minutes, stirring occasionally.
Corn on the cob	Remove husks and silks; rub with butter; wrap in foil.	Bake at 375 degrees for 30 to 35 minutes.
Eggplant	Slice; brush with oil.	Bake at 450 degrees for 20 to 30 minutes.
Onions	Peel; stand upright in baking dish; drizzle with butter.	Bake at 350 degrees for 30 to 45 minutes, basting occasionally.
Peppers (bell)	Place skin side down in greased baking dish; drizzle with oil.	Bake at 375 degrees for 40 to 45 minutes.
Potatoes	Scrub; pierce with fork.	Bake on oven rack at 375 degrees for 1¼ hours.
Squash, summer	Cut into halves; seed; place cut side down in greased baking dish.	Bake at 425 degrees for 30 to 40 minutes.
Squash, winter	Pierce with fork; place on baking sheet with sides.	Bake at 350 degrees for 1½ hours, turning once.
Tomatoes	Cut into halves; core, seed, and juice; arrange cut side up in baking dish; drizzle with oil.	Bake at 400 degrees for 20 to 25 minutes.

Sautéing

The term sautéing originates from the French word sauter, which means to jump. Sautéing is a cooking technique done on top of a stove in a sauté pan (a.k.a. frying pan), with a little fat, over a high heat. The food is continuously stirred or tossed about to prevent it from sticking and/or burning. Sautéing is constantly confused with frying; but in frying, the food is immersed in fat, while sautéing is done in little fat. We often hear the term pan-fry, the American way to say sauté. Again, pan-frying is done in very little fat.

Sauté pans are of course the favorite pan to use when sautéing. The pan usually has 2¹/₂-inch sides and a flat bottom surface, ten, twelve, and sometimes fourteen inches in width. The handles are also longer than most skillets because a lot of shaking and tossing is done when sautéing. Most of these pans also have covers that fit tightly over the top, which is important in some recipes. Sautéing can be done in other pans as well, such as a frying pan, wok, or skillet (especially if it is heavy-duty iron, heavy lined copper, stainless steel, or cast aluminum, with or without Teflon), or a shallow pan with a long handle (and preferably a cover). Most of the simplest forms of sautéing are done without a cover. Covers are good for final browning, reducing a sauce, or keeping the food warm, but they are not essential to the technique.

Sautéing is a process with many options. It's also one of the easiest techniques (next to frying) to complete successfully. Most everyday cooking will fall into this category, either standing alone in this one procedure or combined with another. We sauté everything and anything at any meal. We sauté French toast, scrambled eggs, hash, chicken marsala, pan-fried sole, grilled cheese, and cherries jubilee. Just about anything cooked in the frying pan that adds a little fat (butter, oil, etc.) to cook the food in is sautéed.

Another popular form of sautéing is stir-frying in a wok. A wok, the primary cooking vessel of Asia, has a rounded shape and a long sloped side to provide an extended cooking surface. It can be heated to a very high temperature with very little fuel (fuel being the heat source). You may not think of stir-frying as a form of sautéing but rather frying, due to its name, but it's still a sauté technique done with high heat and little fat. Woks can also be used to braise, deep fry, roast, and boil. They also come with flat bottoms for easier use on a range top and come with Teflon coating; as with any other Teflon product, it's essential not to use metal utensils to stir with, only wood or plastic. Stir-frying has become a popular way to cook many different types of foods, particularly Oriental cuisine.

Stir-frying also denotes a method of cooking bite-size pieces of meat and/or vegetables over a high heat with very little oil or fat. Like anything else sautéed, it is done the same way as if you were doing it in a frying pan. In fact, although stir-frying is a label we put on wok cooking, you can also make a stir-fry in a frying pan.

Stir-Frying Vegetables

Stir-frying is a very quick, delicious way to cook vegetables. However, after stir-frying, you need to add a little water and let them steam briefly.

Vegetable	Fat	Stir-Fry Time	Steaming Time
Asparagus (1/2-inch slices)	1 tablespoon oil	1 minute	2 to 3 minutes
Beans (lima) (1-inch pieces)	1 tablespoon oil	30 seconds	4 to 6 minutes
Beans (snap) (1-inch pieces)	1 tablespoon oil	30 seconds	4 to 6 minutes
Bean sprouts	1 tablespoon oil	30 seconds	1/2 to 1 1/2 minutes
Beets, whole	2 tablespoons butter	1 minute	5 to 6 minutes
Broccoli (florets)	1 tablespoon oil	1 minute	3 to 5 minutes
Brussels sprouts (halves)	2 tablespoons butter	1 minute	3 to 5 minutes
Cabbage (shredded)	1 tablespoon oil	1 minute	3 to 4 minutes
Carrots (1/4-inch slices)	1 tablespoon oil	1 minute	3 to 5 minutes
Cauliflower (1/4-inch slices)	1 tablespoon oil	1 minute	4 to 5 minutes
Celery (1/4-inch slices)	1 tablespoon oil	1 minute	1 to 3 minutes
Eggplant (strips)	2 tablespoons oil	2 minutes	10 minutes
Fennel (1/4-inch slices)	1 tablespoon oil	1 minute	none
Jerusalem artichokes (1/4-inch slices)	2 tablespoons butter	1 minute	3 to 5 minutes

Vegetable	Fat	Stir-Fry Time	Steaming Time
Leeks (white part only) (1/4-inch slices)	1 tablespoon oil	1 minute	3 minutes
Lettuce, iceberg (shredded)	2 tablespoons butter	30 seconds	2 to 3 minutes
Mushrooms (1/4-inch slices)	1 tablespoon oil	3 to 4 minutes	none
Onions (1/4-inch slices)	1 tablespoon oil	1 minute	3 to 4 minutes
Parsnips (1/4-inch slices)	2 tablespoons oil	1 minute	4 to 6 minutes
Peppers, bell (1-inch pieces)	1 tablespoon oil	1 minute	3 to 5 minutes
Peas	1 tablespoon oil	1 minute	30 seconds
Spinach	1 tablespoon oil	30 seconds	2 to 3 minutes
Squash, summer (1-inch cubes)	2 tablespoons butter	1 minute	3 to 5 minutes
Squash, winter (1/4-inch slices)	1 tablespoon oil	1 minute	3 to 4 minutes
Turnips and rutabagas (1/4-inch slices)	1 tablespoon oil	1 minute	4 to 6 minutes
Turnip greens (shredded)	2 tablespoons butter	1 minute	3 to 5 minutes

Sautéing and stir-frying do require a fair amount of preparation. Sautéing is done so quickly that all the ingredients must be ready before cooking. Many sautéed dishes are combined with other raw ingredients to produce a dish. Just as different liquids, broth, or water can be added to ensure tenderness, herbs and spices may be added to the fat to impart flavor to your dish. Many herbs are brought to their full flavor in hot fats. Tender vegetables are often sautéed to improve their flavor and color before being used in soups, side dishes, or entrées. When combining vegetables in a sauté with chicken, allow the chicken to cook halfway before adding the vegetables. This way, the vegetables will add flavor, stay crisp, and not turn to mush. It is not as necessary to brown the vegetables as it is to impart a tender softness to them without their losing color.

Sautéing is one of my favorite techniques because you can do so much with it. The multiples of this process are endless. For instance, a thin fillet of chicken can be made into a number of different dishes just by including different additives. I can sauté the chicken with something as simple as a little garlic and pepper and have a dish. I can also add artichokes and mushrooms, basil, oregano, pepper, and marsala and have another dish. That same chicken can also be sautéed with onions and a little marinara sauce, then garnished with Parmesan cheese, and I have another dish. The contrast of one dish to the other may be as simple as adding a different vegetable. Let's add red peppers, say, to each of the three dishes—well, that simple addition just turned our three dishes into six very differently flavored dishes. Now let's add mushrooms to those six dishes—now

we have twelve different dishes. The list continues and continues, never ending and always changing. The change can be as easy as adding a new herb or spice to a dish: Taste how different dill and tarragon are from each other, totally different. Maybe you want to try a different liquid—this produces different results as well. It doesn't matter what the food is, the combinations of things you can add to that food are endless. This is the reason sautéing is one of my favorite ways to cook.

You can also add a coating of flour to your fish, chicken, pork, lamb, crustaceans, and beef (only tender cuts for sautéing) to make sure the food crisps and browns. You may also wish to coat the food with bread crumbs (as discussed under Frying, page 25) before sautéing to give it a heartier taste or shell.

Sautéing is one of the fastest forms of cooking and has the most leeway to invent all kinds of new combinations. Once you master the technique, you're well on the way to becoming a great cook with lots of options at your fingertips. Remember that practice makes perfect, and like anything else, it takes time to learn the skills and techniques of good cooking.

Let's recap our sautéing technique. First, you must pick a food to cook.

Timely Tip

When sautéing make sure the food is completely dry; otherwise, it will steam and not successfully sauté. Also, never overcrowd the pan because the food will not completely brown (due to the pan temperature dramatically reducing the heat of the fat); it is the hot fat that ensures a crisp, brown coat that prevents sticking.

Sautéing can be done with just about any food you can think of, but the key to sautéing is that the food should be cut thin so that it will cook quickly. Some of my favorite things to sauté are boneless chicken breasts, pork loin, eggplant, shrimp, scallops, fish fillets, zucchini, beef, and even fruits like cherries and bananas. If I were to name all the things you could sauté, it would take up two pages. Another secret to sautéing is that any food can be cut into chunks and strips (thinly sliced). Sautéing should not be a two-hour procedure; most items will only take ten minutes.

Secondly, you need to choose a fat to cook with. I suggest that you use a clarified butter. Clarified butter is made by slowly melting unsalted butter (in order to evaporate excess water), while the milk solids separate and sink to the bottom of the pan. If there is a frothy layer on top of the butter (which should be spooned away), the clear butter in the center of the two deposits is the clarified butter, pure fat and flavor. We use clarified butter because it has a higher burning temperature than regular butter, so it is ideal for sautéing. You may also choose to use a plain or flavored oil. And you may ask, how much fat do I use? There should

be just enough fat to thinly coat the bottom of your pan.

Also, you need to decide if you're going to coat what you are cooking. I almost always try to coat the main sautéing food with flour. For example, I coat the chicken I'm going to sauté, but if I'm going to throw in mushrooms, I wouldn't coat the mushrooms with flour. I may add salt and pepper to the flour for a little flavor—you may want to try some herbs and spices in the flour as well. And if you don't want to use flour, then cook it plain; the purpose of the flour is simply to brown and crisp the food.

Another choice you have when sautéing is whether to add any other ingredients to your dish. You may want to add almonds to the string beans, or mushrooms to the chicken, or maybe you want to add marsala to the chicken, or Frangelico to the string beans. It all sounds confusing, but essentially every time you add an ingredient, you are creating a new recipe. You can add just about anything you can think of. So next time you prepare a recipe, add another ingredient and see what happens. You may just stumble upon a new favorite recipe.

To summarize, start with the pan on the stove, heat the fat, coat the food if desired, and get any additions ready. Start with the food alone in the pan, constantly shaking the pan or stirring; when the main food is about half done, add your additions and then serve.

Check the sautéing recipes for further explanations about sautéing and to get more examples and variations. Since this is a main technique in cooking and is done as a step for so many other cooking techniques, I believe it is the most used and most versatile of all techniques, so have a ball experimenting with it.

Timely Tip

Sautéing is a quick procedure, so make sure the pan you are using is hot and thinly coated with fat. I usually test the fat to see if it is ready by adding just a drop of flour to it. If it bubbles around the flour, then it's ready. Never start heating your pan until all your ingredients are prepared and you're ready to begin sautéing.

Timely Tip

Never add liquor to a pan over the heating element (gas stove, electric stove, etc.). Liquor will ignite at a high temperature, and you don't want that to happen with the bottle over the pan, because it could cause an explosion. The liquor usually will ignite once put back onto the heat. Don't panic; once the liquor has burned off, the flames will die. This happens quickly.

Sautéing Template

1. Prepare the ingredients.
2. Heat the sauté pan (a.k.a. a frying pan) over medium-high to high heat.
3. Add just enough of the selected fat to coat the pan.
4. Add the ingredients to the pan in the order recommended.
5. Toss or stir constantly.
6. Add the seasonings and/or liquids.
7. Serve.

Pepper Parmesan Chicken

serves 2

1 pound boneless skinless
   chicken breast
2 tablespoons flour
2 tablespoons butter or olive oil
2 tablespoons marsala

³/4 cup half-and-half
2 tablespoons grated Parmesan
   cheese
1 teaspoon coarsely ground
   pepper

Trim any excess fat from the chicken. Cut the chicken in half; rinse and pat dry. Flour the chicken, discarding any excess flour. Heat a sauté pan over medium-high heat. Add the butter. Cook the chicken in the butter for 2 minutes per side. Add the wine. Stir in the half-and-half. Add the cheese and pepper.

Cold Cookery

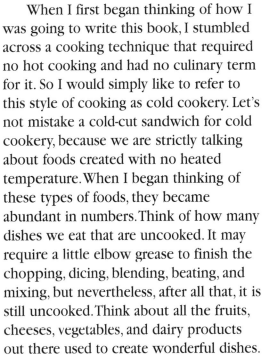

When I first began thinking of how I was going to write this book, I stumbled across a cooking technique that required no hot cooking and had no culinary term for it. So I would simply like to refer to this style of cooking as cold cookery. Let's not mistake a cold-cut sandwich for cold cookery, because we are strictly talking about foods created with no heated temperature. When I began thinking of these types of foods, they became abundant in numbers. Think of how many dishes we eat that are uncooked. It may require a little elbow grease to finish the chopping, dicing, blending, beating, and mixing, but nevertheless, after all that, it is still uncooked. Think about all the fruits, cheeses, vegetables, and dairy products out there used to create wonderful dishes.

Cold cookery will require a wide variety of utensils. Since we are using no pots and pans to cook with, we'll need mixing bowls, cutting boards, a variety of knives, whisks, spoons, and forks, a colander, and more importantly a garbage can and sink nearby. Because we are using raw foods to produce these dishes, there is likely to be more waste (since most of the raw materials have a shell, seeds, or something we need to discard or wash). Everything used in a raw state should be washed thoroughly to remove dirt and/or pesticides.

Again, to avoid food-borne illnesses, always remember to wash the cutting board and knife with hot soapy water before cutting a new food on the same board.

I shouldn't have to tell you but I will anyway: **Always wash your hands!!!!!**

There are soups, chutneys, dressings, entrées, garnishes, desserts, appetizers, drinks, sauces, marinades, dips, and side dishes all done with no cooking. Cold cookery is a vast area of mixing and blending to make an array of dishes from soups to desserts. I hope you find the recipes in the rest of the book helpful in understanding this concept.

So, okay, let's get started.

Horseradish Dipping Sauce

(great for catfish and other fried items)

1/3 cup mayonnaise	1/4 cup chives
1/2 cup sour cream	1 tablespoon garlic
1 1/2 tablespoons horseradish	2 tablespoons lemon juice

Mix all the ingredients together and serve as a side sauce. It's also great as a spread on roast beef sandwiches.

Cold Cookery Template

1. Whisk, blend, or chop the ingredients.
2. Mix the ingredients together.
3. Let stand if necessary.
4. Serve.

Appetizers

Appetizers

Pictured on overleaf (recipe page numbers can be found in the index):

Sun-Dried Tomato Penne, Brownies, Spanish Rice with Black Beans, Creamed Bow Tie Pasta (Florentine-style variation), Chocolate Cream Pie, Apple Pie, Boiled Lobster, Herb-Steamed Steamers (and littleneck and mussel variations), Shrimp Cocktail with Cocktail Sauce, Lobster Cocktail (a variation of Shrimp Cocktail), Whiskey Cake, Tipsy Pudding (a variation of Vanilla Pudding), Tri-Colored Rotini Primavera, Butternut Squash Purée, Black Bean Vegetarian Chili, Roasted Garlic Mashed Potatoes

Inset photos (left to right): Salsa; Grape Mints, Spinach Dip

All these dishes were prepared using the Boiling and Cold Cookery techniques.

Savory Wings

pictured on page 136

1 cup soy sauce
1/4 cup teriyaki
2 cloves of garlic, minced
3 tablespoons brown sugar
1 tablespoon honey

1/4 cup orange marmalade
2 pounds chicken wings,
    preferably with drum and
    wing disjoined

*serves 5, approximately
20 to 30 wings*

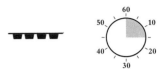

Combine all the ingredients except the chicken and mix thoroughly.
Add the chicken. Marinate in the refrigerator for 2 to 4 hours. Preheat
the oven to 300 degrees. Place the chicken and marinade in a shallow
baking dish. Bake for 1 1/2 to 2 hours, basting and turning the wings
every 15 minutes. Wings should look browned and moist.

Baked Brie

1/2 cup pecans
1 tablespoon butter
1 (1-pound) Brie wheel
    (not sliced)

1/4 cup packed brown sugar

serves 4 to 5

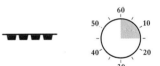

Toast the pecans in the butter for 10 minutes in the oven at 300
degrees. Place the Brie in a quiche pan or pie pan. Cover the top
of the Brie with the brown sugar and pecans. Increase the oven
temperature to 325 degrees. Bake for 15 minutes. Serve with crackers.

Variations

- Before cooking, cover the Brie, pecans and sugar with a pre-made
  puff pastry (remember to put the seam of the pastry on the
  bottom of the pie pan). Bake for an additional 10 minutes or until
  the pastry is golden brown.
- Substitute raspberry jam for the pecans and brown sugar.
- You may even want to try the puff pastry with the jam.

Chicken Liver Pâté

serves 10

10 tablespoons butter
1/2 cup diced onion
2 Granny Smith apples, peeled, diced
1 pound chicken livers
3 tablespoons brandy

3 tablespoons heavy cream
1 teaspoon curry
pinch of nutmeg
pinch each of pepper and salt
parsley
paprika

Melt the butter in a frying pan. Add the onion and apples. Cook until tender. Place in a blender and whip. In the same frying pan, cook the livers for about 5 minutes. Remove the pan from the flame or stove and add the brandy (this may flame if you have a gas burner, so stand back—the flames will subside when the alcohol has cooked off). Combine the livers and the apple mixture in the blender and whip to a smooth consistency. Add the cream and spices and mix well. Pour the mixture out and mold it into a shape. Sprinkle with parsley and paprika (for color). Serve with melba toast or crackers.

Herb-Steamed Steamers

pictured on page 56

serves 4 to 5

1 tablespoon dill
1 small onion, quartered
1 teaspoon oregano
2 cloves of garlic

1 whole bay leaf
2 quarts water
2 pounds steamers
1/2 cup butter

Add the dill, onion, oregano, garlic and bay leaf to the water and bring to a boil. Rinse the steamers just before dropping them into the boiling water. Cover and cook for 8 minutes or until the shells have opened. Drain, reserving 1 cup of the cooking liquid for a rinse dip for the meats of the steamers. Melt the butter and serve as a dip for the steamers.

Variation

- Try this recipe with littlenecks, crayfish, or mussels instead of steamers.

Kiss-Me-Not Stuffed Clams

20 to 25 clams
³/₄ cup chopped fresh garlic
   (about 20 cloves)
³/₄ cup butter, softened
2 tablespoons oregano
¹/₄ cup chopped cooked spinach
¹/₄ cup sherry or white wine

¹/₄ teaspoon nutmeg
¹/₄ teaspoon cayenne pepper
³/₄ cup bread crumbs
¹/₄ cup crushed Ritz crackers
1 egg
1 teaspoon basil
1 tablespoon paprika

serves 5 to 6

Scrub and shuck the clams, reserving the shells. Chop the clams by hand or in a food processor; there should be approximately 1¹/₂ cups. Mix all the ingredients together except the paprika. Stuff the shells (or a simulated-shell dish) with the mixture. Sprinkle the paprika over the top. Bake in a preheated 375-degree oven for 25 to 30 minutes or until the top becomes brown. Serve hot with lemon.

Variations

- Use scallops instead of clams.
- Omit the spinach and add ¹/₄ cup salsa and 2 tablespoons diced green chiles.
- Add ¹/₄ cup pignoli (pine nuts) and substitute chili powder for the paprika.

Smoked Salmon

serves 6

$^1/_3$ cup salt

$^1/_3$ gallon water

3 pounds filleted salmon with
   skin on

$^1/_4$ cup olive oil

Mix the salt and water and pour it over the fish to act as a brine; let stand for 30 minutes. Meanwhile, bring the charcoal grill to flame and burn it almost down; add damp hickory chips against the coals. Rinse the brine from the fish; oil the skin side of the fish. Place the fish skin side down on the grill and cover with the hood. Keep the coals burning with chips for 1 to 2 hours, brushing the top of the fish with oil every 15 minutes. Remove the fish from the grill. Serve warm or cooled with an equal part cream cheese and sour cream dip with dill.

Variation

- Try smoking a like amount of other foods such as chicken, trout, eels, or bluefish. Serve the chicken with lingonberry preserves.

Oops . . . Oops . . . Oops . . . Oops . . .

Make sure the grill is burning and constantly smoking without actually going out. This recipe requires constant attention so that the coals are neither burning nor going out.

Shrimp Cocktail

pictured on page 56

3 pounds peeled deveined shrimp (U12 size)	2 quarts boiling water	*serves 4 to 5*

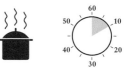

Add the shrimp to the boiling water in a saucepan. Cook for 10 minutes; drain. Place the shrimp in ice water. Drain and serve chilled with cocktail sauce.

Variations

- Add 1 diced onion and 1 tablespoon dill to the water.
- Use 1¹/₂ quarts water and ¹/₂ quart white wine in place of the water.
- Another variation could be to simply serve something other than cocktail sauce as a dipping sauce.

Grilled Shrimp Provençal

pictured on page 10

serves 4 to 5

1¹/₂ cups olive oil
3 cloves of garlic, minced
2 tablespoons oregano
2 tablespoons basil
1 tablespoon dill

1 teaspoon thyme
1 tablespoon parsley
3 pounds larger shrimp, peeled, deveined (15 to 20, preferably)

Combine all the ingredients except the shrimp in a bowl and mix well. Add the shrimp. Marinate in the refrigerator for 2 hours. Remove the bowl from the refrigerator 10 minutes before grilling over medium to high heat. This time allows the oil to desolidify if needed. Before placing on the grill, allow any excess oil to drip off. Should flames flare, move the shrimp to a new spot on the grill. Shrimp cooks quickly and is done when firm to the touch, approximately 3 minutes per side. Serve alone or with cocktail sauce.

Variations

- Use your favorite barbecue sauce as a substitute for the oil, then add the rest of the ingredients.
- Use Italian dressing as a marinade, then add the shrimp.
- Omit the dill and thyme and add ¹/₄ cup grainy mustard.

Creamed Cucumber Boats

pictured on page 76

serves 10

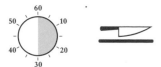

1/4 cup cottage cheese
2 1/2 ounces cream cheese
3 tablespoons sour cream
3 tablespoons whipped topping
    (I like Cool Whip)

1 teaspoon dill
1 small scallion, finely diced
1 long seedless cucumber
cayenne pepper as garnish

Combine all the ingredients except the cucumber and cayenne in a bowl. Cut the cucumber into halves lengthwise. Hollow out the seeds to resemble a boat. Fill the hollows with the cream cheese mixture and sprinkle cayenne over the top. Cut each boat into 1-inch slices and serve chilled.

Oops . . . Oops . . . Oops . . . Oops . . .

If you're having trouble with the filling being too loose, try chilling it for 1 hour first. If that doesn't work, then add a little more cream cheese to the mixture to help solidify it.

Eggplant Martini

serves 4 to 5

1/4 cup peanut oil
1 tablespoon sesame seeds
1 small onion, coarsely diced
1 green pepper, cut into thin
    slices no longer than 1 inch

1 medium eggplant, cut into
    1-inch cubes (leave peel on)
1 shot of gin
1 shot of dry vermouth

Heat a wok or frying pan over medium-high heat and add the oil. Once hot, add the sesame seeds and onion; stir-fry for 3 minutes. Add the pepper. Stir-fry for 3 minutes longer. Add the eggplant. Stir-fry for 5 minutes longer. Remove from the heat to add the gin and vermouth. Return to the heat and cook for 5 minutes. Serve with toasted bagel chips. Great either hot or cold.

Bounty Caps

1 pound mushrooms
  (approximately 20
  mushrooms)
10 tablespoons butter
1 medium onion, diced
2 cloves of garlic, diced
1 tablespoon soy sauce

1 teaspoon crushed red pepper
$1/2$ cup Grape Nuts cereal
$1/4$ cup bread crumbs
8 ounces mozzarella cheese,
  shredded
1 shot of burgundy

serves 4 to 5

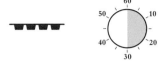

Wash and remove the stems from the mushroom caps and dice the stems. Melt the butter in a frying pan over medium heat. Add the onion, mushroom stems and garlic. Cook for 3 minutes. Add the soy sauce, pepper, Grape Nuts and bread crumbs. Cook until the mixture has absorbed all the liquid, stirring constantly. Remove from the heat. Let cool for 5 minutes before adding the cheese and then stuffing the mushrooms. Place the caps in a baking pan. Bake in a preheated 350-degree oven for 15 to 20 minutes. Remove from the oven. Pour the burgundy into the bottom of the pan immediately and serve.

Variations

- Use $1/2$ cup crushed Ritz crackers instead of the Grape Nuts and add boursin cheese instead of mozzarella.
- Add 6 ounces crab meat, 1 teaspoon dill and 2 tablespoons cream cheese and omit the mozzarella cheese.
- Add $1/3$ cup diced hot cooked sausage, only 4 ounces mozzarella and $3/4$ cup bread crumbs; omit the Grape Nuts.

Spinach Balls

serves 6

2 (10-ounce) packages frozen
    chopped spinach
1/3 cup diced onion
2 cups herb-seasoned crumb
    stuffing
1 cup grated Parmesan cheese

6 eggs
3/4 cup butter, softened
1 teaspoon Tabasco sauce
1 teaspoon basil
1/2 teaspoon pepper

Cook the spinach using the package directions. Combine all the ingredients in a large bowl. Roll the mixture into 1/2-inch balls. Place the balls on a baking tray and freeze (then you can store the frozen balls in a freezer bag or directly bake them on the baking tray). Bake without thawing in a preheated 350-degree oven for 15 minutes. Serve alone or with cocktail sauce.

Oops . . . Oops . . . Oops . . . Oops . . .

If you're having trouble baking the spinach balls because they're falling apart, it is imperative that you allow them to freeze completely. Don't allow them to thaw before you bake them.

Marinated Tomatoes and Garlic Crisps

serves 4 to 5

3 very ripe tomatoes
2 cloves of garlic, diced
1/4 cup olive oil
6 fresh basil leaves, diced
1 teaspoon oregano

1 Ovaline ball of fresh
    mozzarella, diced
1 box garlic hard bread, or thinly
    sliced French bread

Mix all the ingredients in a bowl except the bread. Marinate in the refrigerator for at least 2 hours (I let mine sit overnight). Serve on a platter with bread slices around the rim.

Vegetable Tempura

pictured on page 92

3 egg yolks
2 cups cold water
2¹/₂ cups flour
peanut oil
¹/₄ pound green beans

1 sweet potato, sliced ¹/₄ inch
 thick
¹/₄ cup halved mushrooms
¹/₄ cup broccoli florets

serves 6 to 8

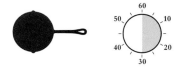

Whisk the egg yolks and water together and slowly add the flour, whisking from the bottom of the bowl up. Stir enough to thoroughly mix, but don't overmix. Preheat the oil in a fryer to 400 degrees. Dip the vegetables in the batter and fry until golden brown (about 5 minutes). Serve with tempura sauce or soy sauce mixed with gingerroot.

Variations

- Add peeled deveined shrimp to make **Shrimp Tempura.**
- Add boneless chicken strips to make **Chicken Tempura.**
- Add a variety of different vegetables.
- Try adding strips of a fish fillet, such as halibut, grouper, mahi-mahi or flounder.
- Another variation could be as simple as using a different sauce or even a relish.

Oops . . . Oops . . . Oops . . . Oops . . .

If the vegetables are sticking together, then you have overcrowded the fryer. Cook in smaller batches. If they are coming out greasy, make sure that between batches you are allowing the oil to come back up to temperature before dropping in the next batch.

Sun-Dried Tomato Penne

serves 6

1 pound penne pasta (the pasta shape really doesn't matter but string pastas are not recommended if using as an appetizer)

$^1/_3$ cup olive oil

$^1/_4$ cup diced shallots

3 tablespoons chopped garlic

3 medium tomatoes, finely diced

$^1/_4$ cup chopped oil-pack sun-dried tomatoes

2 tablespoons chopped fresh basil

1 tablespoon fresh oregano

1 shot of red wine

Boil the pasta in water for about 8 minutes (only 4 to 5 minutes if it's fresh pasta) or until it's just about cooked. Drain the pasta and rinse it in cold water. Toss the pasta with 1 tablespoon of the oil and set aside. Combine the remaining ingredients in a frying pan. Sauté for 4 minutes and then add the pasta. Toss together for 2 minutes and serve. This can be served hot or cold.

Variations

- Try serving this as an entire dinner, or as a cold side salad.
- Try adding $^1/_4$ cup cream to the dish before mixing in the pasta.

Oops ... Oops ... Oops ... Oops ...

If your pan's too small to combine the pasta and the sautéed mixture, simply use a large bowl to mix the 2 together and then serve.

Fried Plantains

pictured on page 92

vegetable oil
3 plantains

1 teaspoon ground cinnamon
(optional)

serves 6

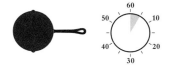

Fill a deep fryer or heavy saucepan with oil and heat to 375 degrees. Peel and slice the plantains into 3/4-inch slices. Add the plantains to the oil and cook for 4 minutes (until brown on both sides). Drain on a paper towel and then flatten the cooked plantain between sheets of waxed paper. Fry again until crisp (another 2 minutes). Sprinkle with cinnamon and serve hot. These are also great dipped plain in honey.

Porkies Texas Biscuits

1 cup Bisquick baking mix
1/3 pound ground hot
sausage, slightly cooked,
drained

5 ounces Cheddar cheese,
shredded
2 tablespoons diced hot green
chiles

serves 6 to 8

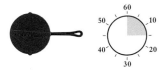

Prepare the baking mix using the package directions. Mix with the remaining ingredients and roll into small balls. Preset the fryer to 325 degrees. Drop in the balls and fry until golden brown (about 6 minutes). Serve with salsa and sour cream.

Broiled Goat Cheese Crisps

1 large onion, sliced
1 tablespoon butter
4 ounces goat cheese
pinch of pepper

pinch of basil
1/2 loaf French bread, sliced into
1/4-inch rounds
3 tablespoons olive oil

serves 4

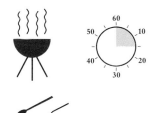

Sauté the onion in the butter until the onion is almost clear; set aside to cool. Mix the goat cheese, pepper, basil and nion in a bowl; set aside. Arrange the sliced bread on a baking sheet; brush the oil over the tops. Cover with the cheese mixture. Broil 4 inches from the top of the broiler for 4 to 5 minutes, or just long enough to brown the exposed edges of the bread. Serve as is.

Grilled Barbecue Pizza

pictured on page 10

serves 4

1 (4-ounce) package pre-made dough (found in a bag at your local grocer's, usually in the dairy section)
2 tablespoons olive oil

1/2 cup barbecue sauce
1 cup Cheddar cheese
1 teaspoon chili powder
1 teaspoon oregano

Start your grill, charcoal or gas, and heat it to medium-high (just past the full heat period on a charcoal grill). Roll out the dough and place on a pizza pan or baking sheet. Brush the oil over both sides of the dough. Let the dough rise as directed on the package. Take the baking sheet out to the grill and place the dough directly on the grill. Let 1 side of the dough cook for about 2 to 3 minutes or just long enough to form a crust on the bottom; flip the dough with a pair of tongs. Brush on the barbecue sauce, add the cheese and sprinkle with the chili powder and oregano. Cook the dough just long enough to melt the ingredients on top or until the bottom of the dough is cooked. Remove from the grill with a spatula. Cut into slices and serve.

Variation

- This is just like making a pizza; try it with marinara instead of barbecue sauce and top it with mozzarella instead of Cheddar. Top it as you would if you were ordering the pizza.

Oops . . . Oops . . . Oops . . . Oops . . .

To make sure the pizza isn't so doughy that it won't cook, make sure you stretch it out really well. If your pizza is burning, then the heat is on too high.

Calzone

1 (4-ounce) package pre-made
   dough
1/4 cup barbecue sauce
1/2 cup diced onion

12 fresh basil leaves
1 cup sliced mushrooms
3/4 cup shredded Cheddar cheese

serves 5

Stretch the dough out as much as you can without breaking it. Place the dough on a baking sheet. Let stand for about 15 minutes or as directed on the package. Mix the remaining ingredients in a bowl and spread evenly over the dough. Roll the dough like a cigar, pressing the seams together with your fingers. Place the rolled dough on a baking sheet; place the baking sheet in a preheated 350-degree oven. Bake until golden brown, about 40 minutes. Let it cool for 15 minutes and then slice and serve.

Variation

- The stuffing in this bread can be just about anything you want and about as much as you want, within reason of course. A good clue that you have overstuffed it is that you cannot roll the dough without tearing it. Here are just a few options for stuffing the dough: ham and cheese; cooked sausage, mozzarella and tomato sauce; fresh oregano, broccoli and mushrooms; cooked chicken, onions and Dijon mustard.

Jalapeño Quesadilla

serves 4 to 5

¹/₄ cup sliced jalapeños (mild or hot, your choice)
2 tablespoons salsa
1 tablespoon diced green chiles
1 scallion, diced
2 tablespoons butter
2 (10-inch) flour burrito shells

¹/₄ cup shredded Monterey Jack cheese
3 tablespoons shredded Cheddar cheese
1 tablespoon sour cream
1 tablespoon guacamole

Mix the jalapeños, salsa, chiles and scallion in a bowl and set aside. Melt the butter in a sauté pan over medium-high heat. Place 1 burrito shell on top of the butter in the sauté pan. Cover the shell with both cheeses, then use the salsa mixture to spread over the cheese. Top with the other burrito shell. When the bottom shell begins to harden, flip the whole quesadilla over very carefully. Let the top shell brown. Once both sides are browned (approximately 4 minutes per side), remove from the heat. Slice like a pizza and serve with sour cream and guacamole in the center.

Variations

- Add ¹/₄ cup cooked chicken and reduce the amount of jalapeños used to 1 tablespoon.
- Add ¹/₄ cup sautéed mixed vegetables of your choice and omit the jalapeños.
- To make a plain **Cheese Quesadilla,** use ¹/₄ cup Cheddar and omit the jalapeños.

Oops . . . Oops . . . Oops . . . Oops . . .

Here's a tip if you're having trouble flipping the quesadilla: Place a plate on top of the sauté pan and transfer the quesadilla over onto the plate. Then slide the quesadilla uncooked side down from the dish back into the pan to continue cooking.

Garlic Parmesan Rolls

pictured on page 136

2 tablespoons chopped garlic
1/4 cup melted butter
3/4 cup grated Parmesan cheese

3 tablespoons chopped parsley
1 dozen pre-made cooked dinner
  rolls

serves 6

Heat the garlic and butter over low heat just until the butter melts.
Add the Parmesan and parsley. Pour into a large zip-top plastic bag.
Add the rolls 1 at a time and shake until coated. Serve the rolls.

Kickin' Guacamole

1 cup diced peeled avocado
1 tablespoon chopped garlic
1/4 cup finely chopped green bell
  pepper
1/4 cup finely diced chives

3 tablespoons salsa
1 tablespoon chopped fresh
  cilantro
3 tablespoons hot sauce
3 tablespoons lemon juice

makes about 2 cups

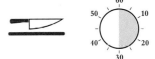

Mix all the ingredients together. Serve with tortilla chips. This can be
refrigerated, but try not to prepare it too far in advance because it is
best served fresh.

Mexi Bean Dip

serves 10

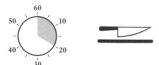

1 (10-ounce) can jalapeño
　　bean dip
3/4 to 1 cup mashed peeled
　　avocados
1 tablespoon lemon juice
pinch of pepper
1/2 cup sour cream
1/4 cup mayonnaise or yogurt

1/2 (1 1/4-ounce) package taco
　　seasoning
1/4 cup sliced olives
1/2 cup diced scallions
1/2 cup diced tomato
1/2 cup shredded Cheddar cheese
1 teaspoon chili powder
tortilla chips

Spread the bean dip in an 8-inch pie plate. Mix the avocados, lemon juice and pepper in a bowl. Spread over the bean dip. Mix the sour cream, mayonnaise and taco seasoning. Spread over the avocado mixture. Layer the olives, scallions, tomato and cheese over the sour cream mixture. Sprinkle with the chili powder. Chill until serving time. Bring to room temperature before serving (about 15 minutes). Arrange tortilla chips around the bean dip.

Soy Garlic Dip

makes about 2 cups

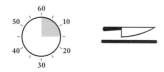

1/4 cup roasted garlic pulp
1/4 cup finely diced chives
8 ounces cream cheese, softened

1 cup shredded Cheddar cheese
1/4 cup soy sauce
1 tablespoon sour cream

Mix all the ingredients together. Serve with vegetables.

Variations

- Spread on French bread and broil until bubbly. Slice to serve.
- Roll steamed potatoes in this dip—a great seasoning.
- It's great when rolled in hot pasta.
- It can also be used to top steamed fresh vegetables.

Kahlúa Dip

pictured on page 76

8 ounces cream cheese
(preferably Temptee brand),
softened
1/4 cup Kahlúa

2 tablespoons evaporated milk
2 tablespoons sugar
3 tablespoons sliced almonds

makes about 2 cups

Mix all the ingredients together until smooth. Serve with sliced
apples, pineapple and strawberries.

Spinach Dip

pictured on page 76

1 cup drained, thawed frozen
chopped spinach
8 ounces cream cheese, softened
1/4 cup sour cream

1/2 package Lipton onion soup
mix
splash of Worcestershire sauce

makes about 2 cups

Mix all the ingredients together. Serve with melba rounds.

Salads & Soups

Salads & Soups

Pictured on overleaf (recipe page numbers can be found in the index):

Pineapple Lime Salad (a variation of Basic Gelatin Mold), Kahlúa Dip, Cold Raspberry Soup (a variation of Cold Yogurt Soup), Creamed Cucumber Boats, Spinach Dip, Grape Mints, Traditional Salsa, Pepper Parmesan Dressing used as a dip, Honey Curry Dressing used as a dip, Texas Corn Salad

Inset photos (left to right): Sun-Dried Tomato Penne; Black Bean Vegetarian Chili

All these dishes were prepared using the Cold Cookery and Boiling techniques.

Basic Gelatin Mold

pictured on page 76

1 (3-ounce) package gelatin   ³/₄ cup boiling water

serves 8

Variations

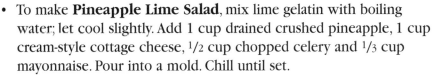

- To make **Pineapple Lime Salad**, mix lime gelatin with boiling water; let cool slightly. Add 1 cup drained crushed pineapple, 1 cup cream-style cottage cheese, ¹/₂ cup chopped celery and ¹/₃ cup mayonnaise. Pour into a mold. Chill until set.
- To make **Strawberry Cream Salad,** mix strawberry gelatin with boiling water; let cool. Mix in one 10-ounce package frozen strawberries, 1 sliced banana, 1 cup chopped walnuts and 1 cup sour cream. Pour into a mold. Chill until set.
- To make **Cran-Orange Mold,** mix orange gelatin with boiling water; let cool. Combine half the gelatin, ¹/₂ cup frozen cranberries and 2 peeled and sliced oranges. Pour into a mold and let cool. Mix the remaining gelatin, ¹/₂ cup lemon yogurt and 2 tablespoons honey. Pour into the mold. Chill until set.

Grape Mints

pictured on page 76

2 cups seedless green grapes
2 cups red seedless grapes
2 tablespoons honey
¹/₄ cup cider vinegar

1 cup mint jelly
2 tablespoons chopped mint
   leaves

serves 4

Cut half the green grapes and half the red grapes into halves. Mix the grape halves, whole grapes and remaining ingredients together. Chill until serving time. This is a great filling for a carved-out watermelon or cantaloupe.

Broccoli Pasta Salad

serves 8

1 bunch broccoli, washed, cut into bite-size pieces (about 2 cups)

³/₄ pound tri-colored rotini pasta

¹/₄ cup soy sauce

3 tablespoons chopped fresh garlic

2 tablespoons chili oil

¹/₄ cup cider vinegar

1 tablespoon honey

¹/₃ cup sesame seeds

¹/₄ cup pine nuts

¹/₂ cup chopped scallions

Steam the broccoli for about 3 minutes (just until partially cooked). Cook the pasta until done; drain and let cool. Mix all the ingredients in a bowl. Chill until serving time. Serve cold.

Variations

- Variations could be as simple as using a different pasta, or roasting the pine nuts and sesame seeds in the oven.
- Add 1 cup cooked shrimp and serve **Broccoli and Shrimp Pasta Salad** as an entrée.

Marinated Vegetable Salad

serves 6

³/₄ cup olive oil

¹/₃ cup balsamic vinegar

1 tablespoon each chopped garlic, oregano, basil and parsley

1 cup bite-size zucchini chunks

1 cup quartered mushrooms

1 (6-ounce) can quartered artichoke hearts

1 pint cherry tomatoes

¹/₂ cup black olives

Timely Tip

Marinades are a great treat to spice up that same old favorite. Give it a try with just about anything: tofu, chicken, beef, pork, lamb or vegetables.

Mix all the ingredients together. Let stand overnight to absorb the marinade. May serve on a bed of lettuce.

Variations

- You can use this marinade (everything except the vegetables) for all kinds of salads—try it with fresh green beans and ¹/₄ cup sliced almonds. Or try a vegetable medley of your own favorites, or try it with fresh mozzarella diced into it. Or use the same ingredients, but grill the vegetables and then mix them in.

Mexi Bean and Rice Salad

1/2 cup diced red onion
1 tablespoon chopped garlic
1/3 cup diced green pepper
1/4 cup diced celery
1 teaspoon yellow mustard
3 tablespoons olive oil
3 tablespoons cider vinegar

1 teaspoon chili powder
2 cups cooked chicken-flavored
  rice
1 cup cooked kidney beans
1 cup cooked garbanzo beans
1/2 cup cooked green beans

serves 6

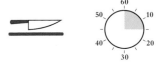

Mix all the ingredients except the rice and beans. Add the rice and beans and mix gently. Chill until serving time. Serve cold.

Texas Corn Salad

2 cups fresh corn kernels
1/2 cup diced tomatoes
2 tablespoons cilantro
1/2 cup diced scallions
1/4 cup olive oil

2 tablespoons cider vinegar
1/4 cup chopped chiles
1/4 cup finely diced celery
1 tablespoon basil
1 teaspoon crushed red pepper

serves 6

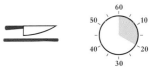

Mix all the ingredients together. Chill overnight. Serve on a bed of lettuce.

Basic Vinaigrette

makes about 2 cups

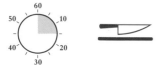

1 cup olive oil or salad oil   ¹/₂ cup vinegar

I prefer balsamic vinegar, but you can also use cider vinegar, wine vinegar or a flavored vinegar.

Variations

- To make **Italian Dressing,** add 1 tablespoon oregano, 1 tablespoon basil, 1 tablespoon garlic powder, 1 tablespoon onion powder, 1 teaspoon thyme, 1 teaspoon marjoram and 1 teaspoon pepper to the base and mix well.
- To make **Dijon Vinaigrette,** add ¹/₄ cup Dijon mustard, 1 teaspoon oregano and 1 teaspoon thyme to the base and mix well.
- To make **Thai Vinaigrette,** mix ¹/₄ cup soy sauce, ¹/₄ cup minced jalapeños, 1 tablespoon cilantro, 1 tablespoon honey and 1 teaspoon crushed red pepper with the base.
- To make **Lemon Pepper Vinaigrette,** add ¹/₄ cup freshly squeezed lemon juice, 2 tablespoons minced lemon peel, 1 tablespoon coarsely ground pepper, 2 tablespoons basil and 2 tablespoons honey to the base and mix well.
- To make **Roquefort Vinaigrette,** mix ¹/₃ cup crumbled Roquefort bleu cheese, 1 tablespoon lemon juice, ¹/₂ teaspoon pepper and 1 teaspoon sugar with the base.

Timely Tip

When making vinaigrettes, remember to always shake or stir before serving to blend ingredients. If you want to emulsify the vinaigrette, simply blend it in a food processor; this will cause it to stay mixed longer.

Basic Mayonnaise-Based Dressing

pictured on page 76

1 cup mayonnaise   ⅓ cup cider vinegar

makes 2 to 2½ cups dressing depending on variation

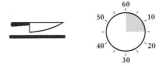

Variations

- To make **Honey Curry Dressing**, mix ⅓ cup honey, ¼ cup curry powder and 2 tablespoons chili sauce with the base.
- To make **Pepper Parmesan Dressing**, add ½ cup grated Parmesan cheese and ¼ cup coarsely ground pepper to the base and mix well.
- To make **Roquefort Dressing**, mix ¾ cup crumbled Roquefort bleu cheese and 2 tablespoons sour cream with the base.
- To make **Honey Mustard Dressing**, add ⅓ cup honey and ⅓ cup Grey Poupon mustard to the base and mix well.
- To make **Dilled Buttermilk Dressing**, add 2 tablespoons dill, ¼ cup buttermilk and 3 tablespoons yogurt to the base and mix well.
- To make **Avocado Dressing**, mix ¾ cup mashed avocado pulp, 1 teaspoon chopped garlic, 1 teaspoon onion powder, 1 teaspoon cayenne pepper and 1 tablespoon lemon juice with the base.
- To make **Poppy Seed Dressing**, mix 1 teaspoon grainy mustard, 2 tablespoons poppy seeds, ⅓ cup sugar (diluted in vinegar) and 2 tablespoons honey with the base.
- To make **Thousand Island Dressing**, add ¼ cup catsup and ⅓ cup sweet pickle relish to the base and mix well.
- To make **Ranch Dressing**, reduce the amount of vinegar to ¼ cup. Mix with the mayonnaise, ⅓ cup buttermilk, 1 teaspoon white pepper, 1 teaspoon finely diced onion and 1 teaspoon minced garlic. (Things you can add to the ranch dressing to zip it up include ¼ cup salsa, 1 teaspoon dill or ¼ cup grated Parmesan cheese.)

Timely Tip

These dressings also make terrific dips for vegetables.

Basic Bisque

serves 6

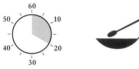

1¹/₂ cups cooking sherry
2 cups chicken-, vegetable-,
   lobster- or clam-based broth
³/₄ cup butter

¹/₂ cup finely diced onions
¹/₃ cup finely diced celery
¹/₂ cup flour
1 cup light cream

Have the sherry and broth simmering in a saucepan over medium-high heat. Melt the butter in a frying pan. Add the onions and celery. Sauté for about 5 minutes over medium-high heat. Add the flour and combine as well as you can (this should only take about 3 minutes). Add to the hot broth mixture. Simmer without boiling for about 20 minutes, stirring constantly. Add the cream just a few minutes before serving.

Oops . . . Oops . . . Oops . . . Oops . . .

If the soup is thicker than you wish, simply add some broth to thin it out. If it's not thick enough, mix equal parts of flour and butter in a frying pan. Add 1 soup spoon of this mixture at a time to the bisque. Let it cook for 10 minutes before adding more until you obtain the consistency desired. This also works for cream soups.

Basic Bisque Variations

Variations

- To make **Lobster Bisque,** use lobster broth or clam juice. At the sauté step, add 2 cups diced lobster meat, 1 teaspoon dill and 1 teaspoon white pepper and continue as directed.
- To make **Roasted Red Pepper Bisque,** use vegetable or chicken broth. At the sauté step, add 2 cups diced roasted red peppers, 1 teaspoon basil, 1 teaspoon oregano and 1 teaspoon white pepper and continue as directed.
- To make **Curried Pumpkin Bisque,** use vegetable or chicken broth. At the sauté step, add one 8-ounce can pumpkin, 2 tablespoons curry powder, 1 teaspoon cinnamon and 1 teaspoon basil and continue as directed.
- To make **Scallop Bisque,** use the same ingredients as the lobster bisque, but use chopped scallops instead of lobster.
- To make **Black-Eyed Pea Bisque,** use chicken broth. At the sauté step, add 2 cups drained cooked black-eyed peas (preferably goya product), 1 teaspoon basil, 1 teaspoon oregano, 1 teaspoon chopped garlic and 1 teaspoon cayenne pepper.
- To make **Cheesy Garlic Bisque,** use chicken broth. At the sauté step, add 1/2 cup Roasted Garlic (see the recipe on page 107) and continue as directed. When you add the cream, also add 3/4 cup shredded White Cheddar. Remember that you're not cooking the cheese; you're just heating enough to melt and incorporate it. Caesar salad croutons are a great garnish for this dish.

Timely Tip

Bisque can be made with just about anything you like, so go ahead and create one of your own favorites.

Basic Broth-Style Soups

serves 6

6 cups chicken, beef, vegetable or
clam stock
1/4 cup butter
1/2 cup diced onions
1/2 cup diced celery

1/2 cup diced carrots
1 tablespoon basil
1 tablespoon oregano
1 teaspoon white pepper

Place broth on the stove over medium-high heat. Melt the butter in a frying pan. Add the onions, celery, carrots, basil, oregano and pepper. Sauté for at least 8 minutes. Add to the broth. Cook over medium heat for 25 minutes.

Variations

- To make **Minestrone,** add 1 cup cooked beans and 1 cup salsa to chicken, beef or vegetable broth. (I like to use pinto beans, but you can use kidney beans or any other you like.) At the sauté step, add 1/2 cup diced zucchini and 1/3 cup diced mushrooms.
- To make **Chicken Noodle Soup,** add 2 cups diced cooked chicken and 3/4 cup of your favorite noodles to chicken broth (I like to use orzo pasta).
- To make **Escarole Soup,** add 1/2 pound (about 1/2 bunch) chopped escarole and 1 tablespoon chopped garlic at the sauté step. You can also add 1 cup diced cooked chicken to this or beans or rice.
- To make **Beef Barley Soup,** add 11/2 cups diced beef and 1 tablespoon garlic at the sauté step and add 1 cup barley to beef stock.
- To make **Chicken Tortellini Soup,** add 1 cup diced cooked chicken and 11/2 cups cooked tortellini to chicken broth.

Basic Creamed Soup

4 cups chicken broth or
   vegetable stock
$1/2$ cup butter
$1/2$ cup diced onions
$1/2$ cup diced celery
$1/4$ cup diced carrots

1 tablespoon basil
1 tablespoon oregano
1 teaspoon white pepper
$1/2$ cup flour
$1/2$ cup light cream

serves 6

Set the broth on the stove over medium-high heat. Melt the butter in a frying pan. Add all the ingredients except the flour, cream and broth. Sauté until the vegetables are tender, about 8 minutes over medium-high heat. Add the flour and mix as well as you can; this may take a few minutes. Add the mixture to the broth. Cook over medium heat for 30 minutes. Don't forget to stir every few minutes. Just before serving, mix in the cream.

Variations

- To make **Creamed Mushroom Soup,** add 2 cups sliced mushrooms at the sauté step.
- To make **Creamed Broccoli Soup,** add 2 cups chopped broccoli at the sauté step. If you want to make it **Creamed Broccoli with Cheese Soup,** add $1/4$ cup grated Parmesan and $1/4$ cup grated Cheddar cheese 5 minutes before serving time. (Remember when adding cheese you just want to melt it, not cook it; if you try to cook it, it will lump and clump up.)
- To make **Creamed Spinach Soup,** add 2 cups chopped spinach at the sauté step and continue as directed.
- To make **Creamed Pumpkin Soup,** add one 8-ounce can pumpkin purée and 1 teaspoon allspice to the broth.
- To make **Creamed Curry Squash Soup,** add $2 1/2$ cups puréed cooked butternut squash, 2 tablespoons curry powder and a pinch of nutmeg to the broth.
- To make **Creamed Potato Leek Soup,** add 2 cups diced peeled cooked potatoes to the broth and substitute $1 1/2$ cups chopped leeks for the diced onions; proceed as directed.

Timely Tip

Hopefully, you get the idea to make a creation of your own!

Black Bean Vegetarian Chili

pictured on page 56

serves 6

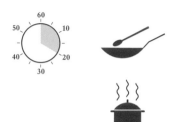

2 (8-ounce) cans precooked
    black beans (preferably Goya)
1 (8-ounce) can cooked red
    kidney beans
1 cup water
1 (8-ounce) can chopped stewed
    tomatoes
3 tablespoons chopped garlic
1 tablespoon crushed red pepper
    (about 3/4 cup)
1 small onion, diced
    (about 3/4 cup)

1 green pepper, chopped
5 tablespoons chili powder
3 tablespoons honey
3 tablespoons brown sugar
1 teaspoon cinnamon
1 teaspoon cumin or coriander
2 tablespoons oregano
2 tablespoons onion powder
1 tablespoon basil
1 cup salsa (your favorite)
Tabasco sauce to taste

Oops . . . Oops . . .

If the chili seems watery, just let it continue cooking until it reduces to the desired thickness.

If it's too thick, simply add water to thin it out. (When I reheat, I will usually add a little extra water anyway.)

If the chili is burning on the bottom of the pan, do not attempt to stir the bottom because this will impart a burned taste. Simply put the ingredients in another pan, but again, don't scrape the bottom. To help clean the burned pan, simply add water to the mess and bring it to a boil. The burned material will slowly loosen.

This is by far the easiest chili to make: just combine all the ingredients in a stockpot and simmer (do not boil) for up to 2 hours (at least 1 hour). Chili should be a rather thick consistency. Serve with a little shredded Cheddar and sour cream. Like most soups, it's always better the second time around.

Variations

- Add a pound of cooked ground chuck to make it a meat-based chili.
- Use the bean mixture as a base on a pizza shell and cover with Cheddar for **Black Bean Pizza.**
- Use the bean mixture as a topping for a salad garnished with tortilla shells.
- Use the bean mixture as a base for **Bean Dip.** Bake in the oven topped with cheese, olives jalapeños, lettuce, tomatoes and sour cream. Serve with chips.

New England Clam Chowder

1/2 cup butter
3 slices bacon, chopped
    (optional)
1 cup diced onions
1/4 cup diced carrots
1 cup diced celery
1 teaspoon dill
1 teaspoon thyme
1 teaspoon basil

1 teaspoon oregano
1/4 cup flour
4 1/2 cups clam juice
3 cups diced potatoes (I like red
    bliss potatoes with the skin
    on)
3 cans diced clams (about 1 cup)
1/2 cup light cream
salt and pepper to taste

Melt the butter in a sauté pan. Cook the bacon in the butter. Add the onions, carrots, celery, dill, thyme, basil and oregano. Sauté for 5 to 10 minutes. Add the flour and mix as well as possible. Add the clam juice and potatoes. Simmer until the potatoes are tender. Add the clams and cream. Cook for 5 minutes. Season with salt and pepper.

Variations

- Omit the flour and cream and add one 8-ounce can chopped stewed tomatoes and 3/4 cup tomato juice to the chowder with the clam juice for **Manhattan-Style Chowder.**
- Omit the flour and cream and it will simply be a broth-based chowder, sometimes referred to as clear chowder.
- Add 1/2 cup chopped spinach to the soup when you add the clam juice for **Florentine-Style Cream Chowder.** Spinach can also be added with the previous 2 variations.
- To make **Corn Chowder,** replace the clams and clam juice with chicken broth and corn. You may also want to omit the dill.

Garlic Soup

serves 5 to 6

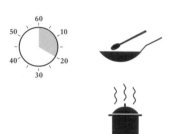

1 stick butter (^{1}/2 cup)
^{1}/2 head of garlic (cloves diced)
1 large carrot, grated (about ^{1}/4 cup)
2 ribs celery, finely diced (about ^{1}/2 cup)
1 small onion, diced (about ^{1}/2 cup)
^{1}/4 cup cider vinegar

2 tablespoons honey
1 teaspoon oregano
1 teaspoon basil
1 tablespoon soy sauce
1 teaspoon crushed red pepper
3 tablespoons flour
4 cups beef broth
2 dinner rolls, cubed

Melt the butter in a sauté pan. Add the garlic, carrot, celery, onion, vinegar, honey, oregano, basil, soy sauce and pepper. Sauté over medium-high heat for 8 minutes. Add the flour and mix thoroughly (this may clump up a bit). Add the beef broth and bread. Bring to a boil and simmer until all the bread has fallen apart (approximately 45 minutes). Serve with garlic croutons.

Classic Onion Soup

serves 6

^{1}/2 cup butter
5 cups thinly sliced onions
(Vidalia onions if in season)
4 cups beef stock
1 tablespoon basil
1 teaspoon pepper

6 slices French bread
^{1}/4 cup shredded Gruyère cheese
^{1}/4 cup grated Parmesan cheese
2 tablespoons shredded mozzarella cheese

Melt the butter in a frying pan. Sauté the onions in the butter until translucent. Set the stock in a stockpot over medium-high heat. Add the basil and pepper. Add the sautéed onions. Cook for 30 minutes. Place the bread slices on a baking sheet and sprinkle with the cheeses. Broil the slices in the oven until bubbly. Ladle the soup into bowls. Top each serving with a piece of broiled French bread.

Turkey Gumbo

1 quart chicken or turkey stock
1¹/₂ cups chopped cooked turkey
1 (8-ounce) can stewed tomatoes
1 cup chopped celery
1 cup chopped onions
1 cup diced chourico
2 tablespoons Tabasco sauce

1 teaspoon red pepper
1 tablespoon oregano
¹/₂ cup salsa
1 tablespoon cilantro (may
    substitute coriander or
    cumin)
¹/₄ cup uncooked rice

serves 8

Combine all the ingredients except the rice in a stockpot. Bring to a boil. Simmer over medium heat. Add the rice. Cook for 40 minutes.

Cold Yogurt Soup

variation pictured on page 76

3 cups yogurt   ³/₄ cup sour cream

serves 6

Combine the yogurt and sour cream in a bowl. Chill thoroughly.

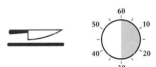

Variations

- For **Cold Cucumber Dill Soup,** add 2¹/₂ cups finely diced or grated seedless cucumber and 1 teaspoon dill and mix well. Chill for at least 20 minutes before serving.
- For **Cold Strawberry Soup,** add 2¹/₂ cups diced strawberries and 1 teaspoon chopped fresh mint and mix well. Chill for 20 minutes. Stir before serving.
- For **Cold Raspberry Soup,** add 2¹/₂ cups chopped raspberries and 1 teaspoon chopped fresh basil and mix well. Chill until serving time.
- For **Cold Peach Soup,** add 2 cups chopped peaches and ¹/₄ cup apricot preserves and mix well. Chill until serving time.

Timely Tip

Cold soups can be made with just about any juicy fruit: pears, blueberries, nectarines, oranges, grapefruit and many more.

Side Dishes

Side Dishes

Pictured on overleaf (recipe page numbers can be found in the index):

Chicken Parmesan, Fried Plantains, Eggplant Parmesan (a variation of Chicken Parmesan), Vegetable Tempura, Fried Eggplant (a variation of Chicken Parmesan), Carolina Fried Chicken

Inset photos (left to right): Broccoli Casserole (a variation of Green Bean Casserole); Grilled Vegetable Kabobs, Grilled Corn

All these dishes were prepared using the Frying, Baking, and Grilling techniques.

Green Bean Casserole

pictured on page 136

1 (10-ounce) can cream of
   mushroom soup
1/2 cup milk
1 tablespoon soy sauce
1 teaspoon ground pepper

2 (9-ounce) packages frozen
   green beans, thawed, drained
1 (3 1/2-ounce) can French-fried
   onions

serves 6

Mix the soup, milk, soy sauce and pepper in a 1 1/2-quart casserole
dish until smooth. Stir in the green beans and half the onions. Bake in
a preheated 350-degree oven for 20 minutes. Top with the remaining
onions. Bake for 5 minutes longer.

Variations

- Try this recipe with frozen chopped broccoli instead of
  green beans.
- Try this recipe with a different type of soup, for example, cream
  of broccoli or cheese soup.

Ginger Broccoli

pictured on page 178

2 tablespoons olive oil
3 cups bite-size broccoli
1/4 cup chopped fresh gingerroot

1 cup chicken broth
pinch of white pepper

serves 4

Heat the oil in a sauté pan over medium-high heat. Sauté the broccoli
and ginger in the oil for 7 minutes. Add the broth and white pepper.
Simmer over medium heat until most of the broth has evaporated.
Serve immediately.

Ratatouille

serves 6

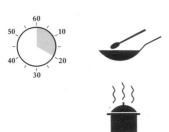

3 tablespoons olive oil
1/2 cup sliced onions
1 cup coarsely diced green
    peppers
1 cup diced zucchini
2 tablespoons chopped garlic

1 tablespoon basil
1 teaspoon oregano
1 1/2 cups diced peeled eggplant
1 (8-ounce) can stewed plum
    tomatoes
1/2 cup diced tomatoes

Heat the oil in a sauté pan over medium-high heat. Add the onions, peppers, zucchini, garlic, basil and oregano. Sauté for 5 to 10 minutes. Remove to a saucepan. Add the remaining ingredients. Simmer for 15 minutes.

Garlic Jalapeño Spuds

pictured on page 136

serves 6

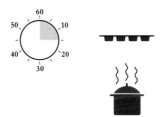

4 cups quartered red bliss
    potatoes
3 tablespoons garlic
1/2 cup diced red peppers
1 stick butter (1/2 cup)

3 tablespoons flour
2 cups milk
2 cups shredded jalapeño Jack
    cheese
1/2 cup seasoned bread crumbs

Boil the potatoes until tender; drain. Combine with the garlic and peppers in a bowl and set aside. Melt the butter in a saucepan. Add the flour and mix as well as possible. Add the milk slowly, stirring constantly. Stir in the cheese. Heat just until the cheese has melted. Mix with the potatoes in the bowl. Place in a baking dish. Top with the bread crumbs. Bake at 350 degrees for 45 minutes.

Oops . . . Oops . . .

If your milk and cheese mixture turns out lumpy, you have cooked the cheese. Remember, the cheese is just supposed to be melted, not cooked. I have no remedy for saving this mess, so try again!

Variations

- Try simply changing the type of cheese; for example, try Cheddar next time.
- Instead of potatoes, use an equal amount of cooked noodles (like macaroni). This makes a great macaroni and cheese.
- Try the noodle variation with a different type of cheese.
- Add 3/4 cup chopped spinach to the cheese and milk mixture for a Florentine-style potato or macaroni.
- Instead of using bread crumbs, try crushed Rice Chex cereal.

Roasted Red Bliss Potatoes

pictured on page 10

5 cups red bliss potatoes,
 quartered (do not peel)
1/4 cup olive oil
3/4 cup sliced onions

1 tablespoon rosemary
1 teaspoon pepper
1 tablespoon garlic
1 teaspoon oregano

serves 6

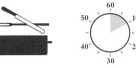

Mix all the ingredients together. Place in a shallow-sided roasting pan. Roast in a preheated 400-degree oven for 40 minutes, turning the potatoes every 15 minutes.

Variations

- Try this with sweet potatoes, or with a mixture of sweet and red bliss potatoes.
- Simply add 3/4 cup grated Parmesan cheese to the top of the red bliss potatoes and roast as directed.

Roasted Garlic Mashed Potatoes

pictured on page 56

4 cups diced peeled potatoes (or
 quartered unpeeled red bliss
 potatoes with skin on)
1/4 cup butter
1/4 cup Roasted Garlic (page 107)

1/4 cup light cream
2 tablespoons chopped parsley
2 tablespoons sour cream
1 teaspoon pepper

serves 4

Boil the potatoes until tender and drain well. Combine with the remaining ingredients in a mixing bowl. Whip with a hand mixer.

Variations

- Add 1/4 cup chopped scallions to make **Garlic and Onion Potatoes.**
- Add 1 cup shredded Cheddar cheese for **Cheesy Garlic Potatoes.**
- Add 1 tablespoon pepper, 1 tablespoon Cajun seasoning and 1/4 cup chopped chives for **Cajun Potatoes.**

The Perfect Baked Potato

pictured on page 178

serves 1

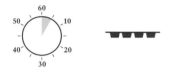

1 baking potato (Idaho potato)

Scrub the potato well under running water. With a paring knife, make a very thin slit around the center of the potato; or prick the potato with a fork 2 to 3 times. Place the potato in the center of the oven rack. Bake in a preheated 425-degree oven for 1 hour or until the potato feels soft.

Variations

- The best variations are the toppings we put on our baked potatoes. Here are some suggestions to try. Go ahead—use as much as you want: sour cream and chives; shredded Cheddar cheese and broccoli; chili and Cheddar cheese; salsa and Tabasco sauce; or butter and sautéed mushrooms and garlic.

Twice-Baked Potatoes

pictured on page 136

serves 6

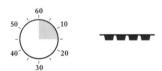

6 large baking potatoes
1/2 cup sour cream
1 stick butter (1/2 cup)
1 cup shredded Cheddar cheese

1 teaspoon pepper
1 teaspoon oregano
1 tablespoon chopped chives
paprika

Wash the potatoes. Make a punctured incision into the potatoes with a fork. Bake in a preheated oven at 350 degrees for 1 hour. Remove from the oven. Cut the potatoes into halves lengthwise. Scoop the pulp into a bowl, leaving the skins intact as thin shells. Mix the potatoes and next 6 ingredients with an electric mixer. Scoop the mixture into the shells. Sprinkle with paprika. Bake in a preheated 400-degree oven for 25 minutes.

Creamed Spinach

serves 6

¹/₄ cup butter
¹/₄ cup diced onions
1 teaspoon basil
1 teaspoon oregano

1 tablespoon chopped garlic
¹/₄ cup flour
1 cup milk
2 cups drained cooked spinach

Melt the butter in a saucepan; sauté the onions in the butter for 2 to 3 minutes. Add the herbs, garlic and flour to make a pasty mixture. Add the milk. Cook over medium heat until thickened, stirring constantly. Add the spinach. Keep stirring because this is a thick cream sauce; you don't want it to burn on the bottom of the pan.

Butternut Squash Purée

pictured on page 56

4 cups diced peeled butternut
    squash
2 tablespoons butter

1 tablespoon brown sugar
1 teaspoon cinnamon
3 tablespoons milk

serves 4

Boil the squash in water until so tender that it almost falls apart; strain off the cooking liquid. Combine the squash with the remaining ingredients in a bowl. Blend with a hand mixer until smooth. Serve immediately.

Variations

- Combine 2 cups chicken broth with the completed purée in a saucepan. Simmer an additional 10 minutes and you have **Butternut Soup.**
- To make **Curried Butternut Purée,** add 2 tablespoons curry powder to the above ingredients and proceed as directed.

Candied Sweet Potatoes

serves 8

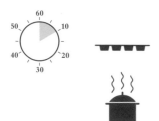

10 sweet potatoes, peeled, cut
　　lengthwise
1 cup dark corn syrup

$^{1}/_{2}$ cup packed dark brown sugar
2 tablespoons butter

Boil the sweet potatoes for 15 minutes; drain well. Mix the corn syrup, brown sugar and butter in a saucepan. Bring to a boil; remove from the heat. Pour half the syrup mixture into a 9x13-inch baking dish. Arrange the potatoes in the dish. Top with the remaining syrup mixture. Bake in a preheated 350-degree oven for 25 minutes.

Creamy Vegetable Casserole

serves 8

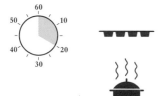

$^{1}/_{4}$ cup butter
1 cup chopped cauliflower
$^{1}/_{2}$ cup sliced zucchini
$^{1}/_{2}$ cup sliced yellow squash
$^{1}/_{4}$ cup diced onion
$^{1}/_{4}$ cup chopped broccoli
5 tablespoons flour
$^{3}/_{4}$ cup milk

1 teaspoon salt
1 teaspoon pepper
1 tablespoon basil
1 cup water
1 egg
1 (8-ounce) package herb-
　　seasoned stuffing mix

Melt 3 tablespoons of the butter in a sauté pan. Add the vegetables. Cook for 5 minutes. Add the flour, stirring to coat the vegetables. Add $^{1}/_{4}$ cup of the milk, stirring to make a paste. Stir in the remaining 1 tablespoon butter, salt, pepper, basil, water, egg and remaining $^{1}/_{2}$ cup milk. Bring to a boil; reduce the heat. Stir in the stuffing mix. Pour into a 2-quart casserole. Bake in a preheated 350-degree oven for 30 minutes.

Grilled Vegetable Kabobs

1/2 cup olive oil
2 tablespoons oregano
2 tablespoons basil
2 tablespoons garlic
1 cup whole mushrooms, washed
1 pint cherry tomatoes

1 cup 1-inch zucchini slices
1 cup 1-inch yellow squash slices
1 cup each quartered cubes of
    yellow, red and green
    peppers

serves 4

Soak a package of wooden skewers in water for 30 minutes. Mix the oil, herbs and garlic together in a bowl. Thread the mushrooms and vegetables onto skewers in any order. Arrange in a pan. Coat with the herb mixture. Place on a hot grill after any excess oil has dripped off. Grill until tender or browned, turning continuously (about 5 minutes on a hot grill).

Variations

- Using the same oil and herb marinade, skewer 1/2-inch-thick sweet potato slices and 1-inch-thick onion slices.
- Add pork, chicken, shrimp or beef cubes to the skewers with the vegetables.

Harvest Roasted Vegetables

pictured on page 10

serves 4

1 cup coarsely diced red peppers
1 cup coarsely diced green
   peppers
1 cup diced peeled butternut
   squash

1 cup diced zucchini
¹/₂ cup coarsely diced onion
2 tablespoons chopped garlic
1 tablespoon basil
¹/₄ cup olive oil

Preheat the oven to 400 degrees. Mix all the ingredients together. Roast for 25 minutes, stirring at least once.

Variations

- Just about any vegetable can be cooked this way. Try different combinations, such as broccoli and red peppers. (Use 2 cups of each with the garlic, basil and oil.)
- Another good combination is 1 cup diced yellow squash, 1 cup quartered mushrooms and 1 cup coarsely diced green peppers mixed with the basil, garlic and oil.

Oops . . . Oops . . . Oops . . . Oops . . .

If your vegetables are getting crisp and brown before the 25 minutes have elapsed, take them out—they're done. If they are not tender and crisp after 25 minutes, allow them a few more minutes to cook.

Grilled Sliced Pineapple

pictured on page 10

serves 3

1 whole pineapple
1 tablespoon olive oil

1 tablespoon mint

Cut the pineapple into 6 slices. Mix the oil and mint and brush onto each pineapple slice. Place each slice on a hot grill. Grill for 1 to 2 minutes per side. Serve immediately.

Creamed Bow Tie Pasta

variation pictured on page 56

serves 4

1 pound bow tie pasta (or any
    pasta you like)
5 tablespoons butter
1/4 cup minced onion
1 tablespoon chopped garlic
1 teaspoon basil

1 teaspoon white pepper
3 tablespoons flour
1 1/2 cups cream (light cream or
    half-and-half)
1/4 cup grated Parmesan cheese

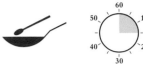

Cook the pasta according to the package directions. Melt the butter
in a frying pan. Sauté the onion, garlic, basil and pepper in the butter
for 10 minutes over medium heat. Add the flour and incorporate as
well as you can. Add the cream. Simmer for 10 minutes. Mix in the
cheese just before serving. Serve when the cheese has melted into
the base sauce. Toss with the cooked pasta. Garnish with parsley
and paprika.

Variations

- For a Florentine-style pasta, add 1/3 cup frozen spinach at the
  sauté step.
- For a zippy cheese sauce, stir in 1/3 cup salsa with the cheese.
- For an added surprise, add 1/4 cup sliced mushrooms and 1/4 cup
  diced peppers at the sauté step; add 2 shots of marsala with
  the cheese.

Timely Tip

To "reduce" a sauce or liquid such as
stock or wine, simply boil rapidly until
the volume is reduced by evaporation.
This process will thicken the consistency
of a sauce and will intensify the flavors.

Oops . . . Oops . . . Oops . . . Oops . . .

If your sauce seems to be very thick, add more cream to thin it
out. If it seems too thin, simply let it reduce over medium to low
heat until it reaches the desired consistency.

Creamy Noodles

serves 6

1 (8-ounce) package noodles
   (I like bow ties)
1/4 cup butter
1 envelope Italian salad dressing
   mix (I prefer Good Seasons)

1/2 cup heavy cream
1/4 cup grated Parmesan cheese

Cook the noodles as directed on the package and drain well. Stir in the butter until melted. Add the remaining ingredients. Toss and serve.

Tri-Colored Rotini Primavera

serves 4

1 (8-ounce) can stewed crushed
   tomatoes
1/4 cup tomato paste
1 tablespoon crushed red pepper
1 tablespoon basil
2 tablespoons oregano
1 bay leaf
1/4 cup water

3 tablespoons butter
1/4 cup diced onions
1/4 cup diced peppers
1/4 cup diced zucchini
1/4 cup bite-size broccoli pieces
1/4 cup chopped mushrooms
1 pound rotini pasta (or pasta of
   your choice)

Mix the tomatoes, tomato paste, red pepper, basil, oregano, bay leaf and water in a stockpot. Cook over medium-low heat for 1 hour. Melt the butter in a sauté pan. Sauté the onions, peppers, zucchini, broccoli and mushrooms in the butter over medium-high heat for 10 minutes. Add to the cooked sauce. Cook for 15 minutes. Cook the pasta according to the package directions. Remove the bay leaf from the sauce. Toss with the drained pasta before serving.

Variation

• To reduce cooking time, omit the water, stewed tomatoes and tomato paste; replace with 1 jar of your favorite tomato sauce. Simply heat the sauce, add all the sautéed ingredients and the seasonings, heat through and serve.

Spanish Rice with Black Beans

pictured on page 56

1 cup uncooked converted rice
1/4 cup diced onion
1/4 cup diced green peppers
1 (8-ounce) can black beans
1 (8-ounce) can stewed tomatoes

1 cup water
1 teaspoon chili powder
1 tablespoon oregano
1 tablespoon chopped garlic
1/2 teaspoon saffron (optional)

serves 6

Mix all the ingredients together in a saucepan. Bring to a boil. Reduce to a simmer over low heat. Cover the saucepan and cook for 25 minutes or until the rice is tender.

Sausage and Grits Casserole

1 pound loose hot sausage,
   cooked, drained
3 cups cooked grits (as directed
   on package)
1 1/2 cups milk
3 eggs

3 tablespoons butter
10 ounces Cheddar cheese,
   shredded
1/2 teaspoon pepper
1/2 teaspoon salt
1/4 teaspoon nutmeg

serves 6

Mix all the ingredients together in a large bowl. Pour into a greased casserole dish. Bake, uncovered, in a preheated 350-degree oven for 1 hour.

Apricot Papaya Chutney

pictured on page 10

1 cup chopped papaya
1/2 cup apricot preserves

1/4 cup chopped walnuts
2 teaspoons chopped parsley

makes about 2 cups

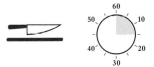

Mix all the ingredients together. Serve with cheese, crackers, fish and/or chicken (serve just like you'd serve applesauce or cranberry sauce).

Chili Pineapple Chutney

makes about 2 cups

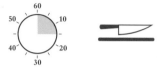

1 cup crushed pineapple
1/4 cup diced green chiles

1/4 cup jalapeño jelly
1/2 teaspoon chili powder

Mix all the ingredients together. Serve with cheese, crackers, fish and/or chicken.

Cran-Apple Chutney

pictured on page 10

makes about 2 cups

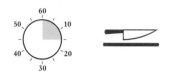

3/4 cup frozen cranberries
1 cup finely diced Granny Smith
  apples
1 teaspoon cinnamon

1/4 cup chopped pecans
2 tablespoons brown sugar
2 tablespoons cider vinegar
1/2 cup applesauce

Mix all the ingredients together. Serve like the above chutneys.

Star Peach Chutney

pictured on page 10

makes about 2 cups

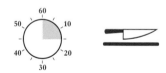

1/2 cup sliced star fruit
1/2 cup diced peaches

1/2 cup peach preserves
1/2 cup red seedless grapes

Mix all the ingredients together. Serve like the above chutneys.

Roasted Garlic

1 head garlic

makes variable amount

Cut off the top third (not the root part) of the head of garlic. Place the head of garlic in a small baking dish. Roast in a preheated 400-degree oven for 30 to 40 minutes or until the outer skin turns brownish and the center is soft when pressed. Let cool for 10 minutes. Squeeze the entire head from the root up to push the roasted garlic out. May be used as an ingredient in other recipes.

Basic Salsa

variation pictured on page 76

1/2 cup finely diced sweet onion (preferably Vidalia)
1 tablespoon chopped garlic

2 tablespoons fresh cilantro
2 tablespoons olive oil

makes about 2 cups with a variation added

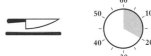

Variations

- To make **Traditional Salsa,** mix 1 1/4 cups diced tomatoes, 1 teaspoon crushed red pepper and 1 tablespoon chopped chiles with the base.
- To make **Mango Salsa,** mix 1 cup chopped mangos, 1 tablespoon chopped mint and 1/4 cup chopped scallions with the base.
- To make **Tequila Salsa,** add 1 cup diced peeled oranges, 1/4 cup diced peeled limes, 1 shot of tequila and 1 shot of Triple Sec to the base and mix well
- To make **Avocado Salsa,** add 1 cup diced avocados and 1/2 cup diced tomatoes to the base and mix well.
- To make **Corn Salsa,** mix 1 cup corn and 1/2 cup diced tomatoes with the base.
- To make **Black Bean Salsa,** add 1 cup cooked black beans, 1/2 cup diced tomatoes and 1 teaspoon chili powder to the base and mix well.
- To make **Pineapple Salsa,** mix 1 cup diced pineapples and 1/4 cup maraschino cherries with the base.

Timely Tip

All these salsas are great on baked or grilled fish and chicken, and also alone with crackers.

Meat & Poultry Entrées

Meat & Poultry Entrées

Pictured on overleaf (recipe page numbers can be found in the index):

Brandied Chicken and Black Pepper (a variation of Brandied Filet Mignon and Black Pepper), Chicken Scampi with red and green pepper variation, Sun-Dried Tomato Chicken, Chicken Cashew, Gorgonzola Chicken Sauté, Chicken in Vinegar Sauce, Chicken with mushrooms, artichokes, tomatoes, garlic, and oregano (a variation of Veal Marsala), Chicken Piccata (a variation of Sole Piccata), Hot and Spicy Chicken (a variation of Hot and Spicy Shrimp), Chicken with mushrooms, scallions, basil and roasted red peppers (a variation of Veal Marsala), Mango Margarita Chicken

Inset photos (left to right): Honey and Beer Baked Ham; Roast Lamb, Roast Turkey

All these dishes were prepared using the Sautéing and Roasting techniques.

Roast Beef

variation pictured on page 10

5 pounds roast beef or prime rib   2 tablespoons rosemary
1/4 cup chopped garlic   1/4 cup olive oil
2 tablespoons oregano   1/2 cup diced onion
2 tablespoons pepper

serves 8

Place the beef on a roasting rack. Mix the herbs, oil and onion and spread over the top of the beef. Cook in a preheated 375-degree oven for about 1 hour and 45 minutes for a medium cut of meat at 160 degrees or adjust the cooking time to your preferred doneness using the scale provided. Let cool for 10 minutes before cutting.

Variations

- This can also be done with a leg of lamb.
- Try using a piece of pork, but cook it to a temperature of 165 degrees.
- This also works well with a crown of lamb (ask your butcher to prepare a crown for you).
- Can also be used with a sirloin butt.

Oops . . . Oops . . . Oops . . . Oops . . .

You keep taking out the meat at 160 degrees and it's always overcooked—why? If you want a piece of meat to be a medium doneness at a temperature of 160 degrees, take it out at 150 degrees. The meat will "carryover" cook, which means it continues cooking another 10 degrees after it comes out of the oven.

Roasting Times and Thermometer Temperatures

Rare: 17 minutes per pound or 140 degrees

Medium rare: 19 minutes per pound or 150 degrees

Medium: 21 minutes per pound or 160 degrees

Medium well: 24 minutes per pound or 165 degrees

Well done: 29 minutes per pound or 170 degrees

Yankee Pot Roast

serves 8

2 tablespoons olive oil
3½ pounds boneless beef round
1½ cups quartered onions
1 cup coarsely diced carrots
8 small red bliss potatoes
1 teaspoon pepper
1 teaspoon garlic powder

1 cup catsup
¼ cup Worcestershire sauce
2 tablespoons brown sugar
2 tablespoons cider vinegar
2 cups water
¼ cup melted butter
5 tablespoons flour

Heat oil in a large skillet over medium-high heat. Add the beef. Cook until all sides are brown. Place the beef in a large saucepan or roasting pan. Add the onions, carrots, potatoes, pepper, garlic powder, catsup, Worcestershire sauce, brown sugar, vinegar and water. Simmer over medium heat. Cover the pan and simmer for 3 hours. Remove the beef to a serving tray and slice. Remove the vegetables and arrange around the sliced beef. Heat the broth in a saucepan. Stir in a mixture of the butter and flour. Heat until thickened. Serve gravy on the side.

Brandied Filet Mignon and Black Pepper

variation pictured on page 108

serves 1

2 tablespoons clarified butter or
    olive oil
2 teaspoons ground pepper

1 (8-ounce) filet mignon
2 tablespoons brandy
¼ cup half-and-half

Heat the butter or oil in a sauté pan over high heat. Press half the pepper into each side of the filet to coat the beef. Place the filet mignon in the sauté pan. Cook for 4 minutes and turn the steak. Remove from the heat. Add the brandy and return to the stove. Be careful: If you have a gas stove, it may flame, but it will go out when all the alcohol has burned off (about 1 minute). Add the half-and-half. Cook until reduced and creamy in texture (about 1 minute). Serve whole or sliced with the sauce on top.

Variations

- This is a terrific dish when made with 8 ounces boneless chicken instead of beef. Follow the above directions.
- It is also great with sliced veal or boneless pork chops (loin cut).

Grilled Steaks

pictured on page 10

1 (10-ounce) steak (filet mignon,
    T-bone, rib-eye, porterhouse,
    etc.)

serves 1

Broil the steak in the oven or cook on a hot grill for 3 minutes per side for a medium steak. For best results use a thermometer and cook to the desired doneness using a temperature guide. Steaks are great alone, basted with barbecue sauce or topped with butter.

Steak Diane

1 (10-ounce) sirloin
1¹/₂ tablespoons butter
1 tablespoon Cognac

2 tablespoons sherry
1 teaspoon chives
1 tablespoon butter

serves 1

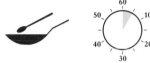

Heat a sauté pan until very hot. Trim the fat from the steak. Cover the steak with plastic wrap and pound it flat with a mallet or the bottom of a saucepan. Add the butter to the hot sauté pan. Add the steak. Cook for 2 minutes per side. Remove from the heat and add the Cognac and sherry. Return to the heat. Be careful if you have a gas stove—it may flame until the alcohol is burned off. Add the chives and 1 tablespoon butter. Serve straight from the pan.

Variations

- This can be done with a floured boneless skinless chicken breast, a floured pork cutlet, or even with scallops and shrimp.
- You may add ¹/₂ cup sliced mushrooms to the sauté pan after you first turn the steak.

Enchiladas

serves 6

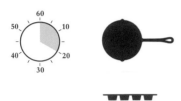

1 pound ground beef or ground
   turkey
1 (16-ounce) can tomatoes
1 (6-ounce) can tomato paste
1¼ cups water
2 tablespoons chopped garlic
¼ cup chili sauce

½ cup chopped onion
2 tablespoons chili powder
1 teaspoon red pepper flakes
1 tablespoon oregano
¼ cup olive oil
1 (8-ounce) package tortilla shells
2 cups shredded Cheddar cheese

Sauté the ground beef until brown and crumbly. Drain and return to medium heat. Add the tomatoes, tomato paste, water, garlic, chili sauce, onion, chili powder, pepper flakes and oregano. Heat the oil in a sauté pan over medium heat. Place the tortilla shells in the oil 1 at a time. Cook each for 1 minute per side. Remove the shells quickly. Scoop some of the tomato and beef mixture with a pinch of the cheese into each shell. Roll up tightly (like a cigar) and place seam side down in a baking dish. Top with any remaining tomato mixture and cheese. Cover with aluminum foil. Bake in a preheated 375-degree oven for 25 minutes.

Variations

- Try this recipe with 1 pound chopped cooked chicken used like the ground beef.
- Try this with 1 pound peeled, deveined shrimp.
- Try this with 2 cups of sautéed vegetables of your choice instead of meat; or add 1 cup of mixed vegetables to the ground beef.
- To make the burrito with any of these variations, don't fry the tortilla—simply roll it and top it with a little enchilada sauce. The dish will not need to be covered with foil.

Oops . . . Oops . . . Oops . . . Oops . . .

If you are having trouble rolling the tortilla shells after frying them, you're cooking them too long. If your shells are not crisp when they come out of the oven, you didn't fry them long enough beforehand. It takes a little practice, so don't be discouraged the first time you try this.

Ground Beef and Eggplant Casserole

12 (¹/₂-inch-thick) peeled
   eggplant slices
2 pounds ground beef
2 tablespoons olive oil
¹/₄ cup chopped onion
¹/₄ cup chopped green pepper
2 tablespoons flour

2 teaspoons oregano
1 teaspoon black pepper
1 teaspoon red pepper
2 cups spaghetti sauce
1¹/₂ cups shredded Cheddar
   cheese

serves 6

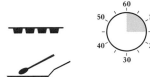

Preheat the oven to 300 degrees. Boil the eggplant in enough water to cover for about 5 minutes or until tender; drain. Brown the ground beef in a sauté pan, stirring until crumbly; drain any excess fat. Add the oil, onion, green pepper, flour, oregano, black pepper, red pepper and spaghetti sauce and mix well. Layer the eggplant, ground beef mixture and cheese ¹/₂ at a time in a buttered casserole dish. Bake for 35 minutes or until the cheese is melted and bubbly.

Timely Tip

To avoid discoloration, eggplant should always be cut just before using.

Lasagna

pictured on page 136

serves 8

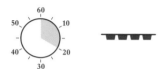

4¹/₂ cups spaghetti sauce
1 pound ricotta cheese
8 ounces mozzarella cheese,
  shredded
1 cup grated Parmesan cheese
1 large egg

2 tablespoons oregano
8 ounces uncooked lasagna
  noodles
1 pound ground beef, cooked,
  drained

Spread 1 cup of the spaghetti sauce in a greased 9x13-inch baking pan. Mix the three cheeses, egg and oregano in a bowl and set aside. Arrange a layer of uncooked lasagna noodles over the sauce in the pan; spread with the cheese mixture and ¹/₂ cup spaghetti sauce. Press another layer of lasagna noodles in the opposite direction over the sauce and cheese. Place the cooked ground beef over this layer. Top with 1 cup spaghetti sauce and another layer of noodles. Again layer noodles in opposite directions so each layer of noodles criss-crosses one another. Add the remaining 2 cups spaghetti sauce over the noodles. Sprinkle with additional grated Parmesan cheese (this is optional). Bake in a preheated 350-degree oven for 1 hour. Let cool for at least 15 minutes before cutting into pieces.

Variations

- Instead of the beef layer, try a layer of sautéed vegetables such as ¹/₂ cup mushrooms, ¹/₂ cup zucchini, 2 tablespoons garlic and ¹/₂ cup spinach.
- Instead of the beef, try 1 pound diced, cooked chicken.
- Or simply omit the beef altogether, and just have a cheese lasagna.

Stuffed Peppers

3 pounds ground beef or
   ground turkey
1 cup sour cream
1 1/2 cups seasoned bread crumbs
1 envelope Lipton onion
   soup mix
2 small eggs

1 teaspoon basil
1 tablespoon oregano
1 teaspoon pepper
3 to 4 large whole green peppers
1 cup premade tomato sauce
   (8-ounce jar spaghetti sauce)

serves 6

Preheat the oven to 350 degrees. Combine all the ingredients except the green peppers and tomato sauce in a large bowl. Cut the peppers into halves (through the stem) and remove the seeds. Place the peppers open end up in a baking dish sprayed with Pam. Fill the peppers with the meat mixture and top with the tomato sauce. Bake for 1 hour. Let cool for 5 minutes before serving.

Variations

- Try different meats—ground beef, ground turkey or ground chicken. Each adds its own unique flavor to the dish.
- You can omit the peppers and make 1 meat loaf. If you do this, cook it for an additional 15 minutes. (It will fit in a 6-cup loaf pan.)
- Try topping each of the variations with diced bacon and no sauce; then try it with the sauce, or simply with nothing at all on it.
- This recipe (without the peppers and the sauce) can be made up into patties for burgers and then pan fried on the stove or grilled on the grill. If you're grilling, add a little barbecue sauce for zip. These are great on the hibachi for tailgating.

Braised Veal Shanks

serves 3

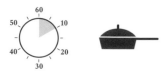

4 pounds veal shanks (3 pieces)	1/2 cup chopped carrots
3 tablespoons flour	1 teaspoon thyme
3 tablespoons olive oil	1 teaspoon oregano
1/2 cup chopped onion	1 teaspoon minced garlic
1/2 cup diced celery	2 cups beef stock

Dredge the veal shanks in flour. Sauté in the oil in a frying pan until the outside has browned (about 2 minutes per side). Place the shanks in a braising pot or large casserole dish. Add the remaining ingredients and cover tightly. Bake in a preheated 300-degree oven for 1 1/2 hours. Serve with the vegetables on top of the shanks with a spoonful of pan drippings over each.

Roast Veal with Mustard Tarragon Sauce

serves 4

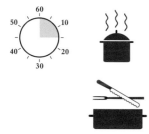

1 1/2 pounds boneless shoulder or top sirloin of veal	1/3 cup chopped celery
2 tablespoons olive oil	3/4 cup chopped onion
1 teaspoon Dijon mustard	1 tablespoon tarragon
1 teaspoon pepper	1/3 cup chicken stock
1 teaspoon tarragon	2 teaspoons Dijon mustard
1/3 cup chopped carrots	3/4 cup heavy cream

Preheat the oven to 400 degrees. Place the veal in a roasting pan. Rub the veal with the oil and Dijon mustard. Sprinkle with the pepper and tarragon. Arrange the carrots, celery and onion around the veal. Mix the remaining ingredients except the cream in a small bowl. Pour over the veal. Roast until it reaches an internal temperature of 150 degrees, about 1 1/2 hours. Baste every 30 minutes. Place the roast on a serving tray with the vegetables. Pour the pan drippings into a saucepan and add the cream. Bring to a boil; reduce the heat to low. Simmer for 6 minutes. Slice the veal and top it with the cream sauce.

Oops . . . Oops . . .

If your veal has a tendency to burn in the oven, cover it with foil once it has browned to your liking. If your sauce is too thin, add 1 teaspoon cornstarch mixed with 1 tablespoon cold water. If it's too thick, add a little water.

Veal Marsala

pictured on page 136

1 pound veal, cut evenly into thin
slices
1/4 cup flour

3 tablespoons olive oil
1 1/2 cups quartered mushrooms
1/3 cup marsala

serves 3

Pound the veal until very thin. Coat the veal with the flour, discarding any unused flour. Heat the oil in a sauté pan over high heat until very hot. Add the floured cutlets. Cook for 2 minutes and turn. Add the mushrooms. Cook for 2 minutes. Remove from the heat and add the wine. Return to the heat. Cook for 2 minutes. Serve immediately.

Variations

- Simply substitute chicken, pork or eggplant for the veal.
- Try adding 1/4 cup quartered artichokes, 1/4 cup diced tomatoes, 1 teaspoon chopped garlic and 1 teaspoon oregano with the mushrooms.
- Try adding 1/4 cup scallions, 1 teaspoon basil, 1 teaspoon pepper and 1/4 cup roasted peppers with the mushrooms.
- Replace the mushrooms with 1/4 cup sliced onions, 1 teaspoon red pepper, 1 teaspoon oregano, 1/4 cup diced tomatoes and 2 tablespoons salsa.
- Reduce the mushrooms to 1/4 cup and add 1/4 cup banana pepper rings, 1/4 cup roasted red peppers, 1 teaspoon chopped garlic and 1 teaspoon marjoram. Use 1/4 cup grated Parmesan cheese for a garnish when it's done.
- Or use only 1/4 cup mushrooms, 1/4 cup red and green peppers and 1/4 cup diced tomatoes, and garnish with 2 tablespoons grated Parmesan cheese.

Irish Stew

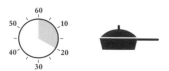

serves 6

¹/₄ cup butter
¹/₄ cup flour
3 pounds lamb shoulder,
    chopped, or breast meat cut
    into 2-inch cubes
2 quarts beef stock
2 cups chopped (1-inch) carrots
3 cups diced (1-inch) potatoes

1 cup pearl onions
¹/₂ cup red wine (optional)
1 tablespoon chopped fresh
    rosemary
1 tablespoon oregano
1 tablespoon basil
1 tablespoon chopped garlic

Melt the butter in a large saucepan over medium heat. Flour the lamb cubes. Sauté in the butter for 3 minutes. Add the excess flour and beef stock. Add the remaining ingredients 1 at a time, stirring constantly. Simmer over low heat for 1 to 2 hours. Add water if there is not enough liquid to cover all the ingredients. Should you want to thicken it a little, melt ¹/₄ cup butter in a small saucepan. Mix in ¹/₄ cup flour and add to the stew. Cook for 10 more minutes (repeat if still too thin).

Variation

- To make **Beef Stew,** simply substitute beef for the lamb and follow the above directions.

Honey and Beer Baked Ham

pictured on page 178

1 (13-pound) ham, whole or
    spiral cut, not canned
15 whole cloves
2 cups water

3/4 cup honey
1 can dark beer (optional)
1 can sliced pineapple (about 10
    slices)

serves 20

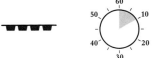

Stud the ham with the cloves. Mix the water, honey and beer in a bowl. Pour the mixture over the ham. Arrange the pineapple on top of the ham. Bake in a preheated 325-degree oven for 15 minutes per pound or until a thermometer registers 160 degrees, basting every 30 minutes.

Oops . . . Oops . . . Oops . . . Oops . . .

If your ham is dry or burned, next time try basting more often. Also, place some foil over the top of the ham halfway through cooking to prevent burning. Your oven may also be running at a higher heat than its reading, so try turning the temperature down by 20 degrees.

Braised Pork Chops with Green Peppercorns

serves 2

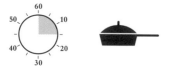

1 pound thin pork chops
1 teaspoon pepper
1/2 teaspoon paprika
1/4 cup flour
3 tablespoons olive oil
1/3 cup chopped carrots
1/2 cup quartered onion

2 tablespoons chopped garlic
1 bay leaf
1/2 cup water
3/4 cup chicken broth
2 tablespoons Dijon mustard
2 tablespoons water-pack
   green peppercorns

Sprinkle the pork chops with pepper. Mix the paprika with the flour and dredge the chops, discarding the excess flour. Heat the oil in a sauté pan over medium heat. Cook the chops for 2 minutes per side or enough to brown. Combine the chops with the remaining ingredients except the Dijon mustard and peppercorns in a large skillet. Cook, covered, over low but simmering heat for 20 minutes. Remove the chops and vegetables to a serving tray. Add the Dijon mustard and peppercorns to the cooking liquid. Remove and discard the bay leaf. Ladle the sauce over the chops and serve.

Barbecued Ribs with Herbs

pictured on page 10

serves 6

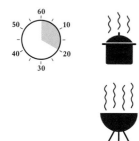

1 cup red wine
1 tablespoon brown sugar
1/2 cup catsup or chili sauce
2 tablespoons soy sauce
2 tablespoons honey
1 tablespoon chopped garlic
1/4 cup vinegar

5 pounds spareribs
1 cup diced onion
1 teaspoon ground cloves
1 teaspoon rosemary
1 teaspoon thyme
1 teaspoon marjoram
1 teaspoon oregano

Mix the wine, brown sugar, catsup, soy sauce, honey, garlic and vinegar in a bowl and set aside. Boil the spareribs with the remaining ingredients for 45 minutes, making sure there is enough water to cover the ribs. Drain the water and pour the wine mixture over the ribs. Chill for about 1 hour. Grill the ribs slowly over hot coals or on a gas grill on medium heat. Grill for about 30 minutes, basting with the excess marinade.

Coq au Vin

1 (5-pound) chicken, cut into 8
    pieces
$^1/_4$ cup flour
$^1/_2$ cup butter
1 cup finely diced ham
2 cups sliced onions
2 tablespoons chopped garlic
1 teaspoon thyme

1 bay leaf
1 teaspoon oregano
1 teaspoon pepper
2 cups whole mushrooms
$^1/_2$ cup Cognac
1 cup dry red wine
$^1/_4$ cup chicken stock

serves 6

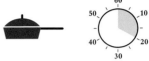

Coat the chicken in the flour; discard any excess flour. Heat the
butter in a sauté pan over high heat. Brown the chicken in the butter.
Remove the chicken to a large casserole dish. Add the remaining
ingredients to the sauté pan away from the heat. Return the pan to
the heat. (Be careful because the Cognac most likely will ignite, so
stand back. The flame will extinguish itself when the alcohol burns
off.) Cook until it comes to a slow boil. Pour over the chicken. Cover
the casserole dish and bake in a preheated 350-degree oven for 1
hour or until the chicken is cooked through. Bake, uncovered, for
15 minutes. Discard the bay leaf.

Crispy Chili Chicken

1 (3-pound) chicken, cut into
    quarters (or 3 pounds legs,
    thighs or breasts)
1 teaspoon pepper
2 tablespoons chili powder
$^1/_2$ cup flour

1 egg
2 tablespoons milk
$1^1/_2$ cups crushed potato chips
    (best done in a food
    processor)

serves 4

Sprinkle the chicken with the pepper and half the chili powder.
Combine the chicken and flour in a zip-top plastic bag. Shake until
the chicken is coated. Discard any excess flour. Whisk the egg and
milk in a bowl. Mix the remaining chili powder with the potato chips
in a flat pan. Dip the chicken into the egg mixture, coating well. Roll
the chicken in the chips, pressing to coat. Place in a single layer in a
shallow baking pan lined with foil. Bake in a preheated 375-degree
oven for 30 minutes. Turn over the chicken. Bake for 30 minutes or
until crisp, browned and cooked through.

Gorgonzola Chicken Sauté

serves 2

1 pound boneless skinless
   chicken breasts
¹/4 cup flour
¹/4 cup clarified butter
¹/2 cup diced onion
¹/2 cup tomatoes
1 teaspoon chopped garlic

¹/4 cup diced scallions
1 teaspoon oregano
¹/2 teaspoon red pepper flakes
¹/4 cup chicken broth
¹/4 cup marsala wine
¹/4 cup crumbled Gorgonzola
   cheese

Trim any fat from the chicken. Cut the chicken into 2-inch strips and dredge in the flour. Discard any excess flour. Heat the butter in a sauté pan over medium-high heat. Add the chicken. Cook for 2 minutes. Turn over the chicken and add the onion, tomatoes, garlic, scallions, oregano and pepper flakes. Cook for 2 minutes. Add the broth and marsala. Cook until the liquid is reduced by half and the chicken is cooked through. Serve topped with the cheese.

Variations

- Substitute sliced veal for the chicken.
- For a different twist, try this with scallops and/or shrimp.
- It's also good when sliced eggplant is substituted for the chicken.

Oops . . . Oops . . . Oops . . . Oops . . .

If your sauce is still too liquid, you can do one of two things: Let it reduce by cooking; or sprinkle in small amounts of flour to thicken it as it cooks (about 1 teaspoon flour at a time). If you are ending up with no sauce at all, simply add a little more marsala and broth to the pan.

Marinated Grilled Chicken

pictured on page 10

serves 2

¹/₂ cup soy sauce
¹/₂ cup pineapple juice
1 tablespoon grated ginger

1 teaspoon pepper
1 pound boneless chicken
   breasts

Mix all the ingredients except the chicken in a bowl. Add the chicken. Marinate in the refrigerator for at least 30 minutes. Remove the chicken from the marinade. Grill over medium-high heat for about 4 minutes per side or until cooked through and firm to the touch. If you prefer broiling, place the chicken in a shallow baking dish with just enough marinade to coat the bottom. Broil in a preheated oven for 8 to 10 minutes or until cooked through.

Variations

- This marinade is great for pork and beef.
- To make the marinade a little more citrusy, add ¹/₄ cup pineapple juice, ¹/₄ cup orange juice and some lemon and lime wedges.

Oops . . . Oops . . . Oops . . . Oops . . .

If your chicken lacks flavor, then it didn't marinate long enough, or the marinade didn't completely cover the chicken. Remember, chicken needs to absorb the marinade. For added flavor, baste the chicken with leftover marinade as it cooks.

Mango Margarita Chicken

serves 2

1 pound boneless skinless
  chicken breasts
1/4 cup flour
4 tablespoons clarified butter
1 cup mango slices (find them
  already sliced in syrup in the
  produce section of your
  grocery)

1/2 cup peeled orange wedges
1 tablespoon basil
3 tablespoons tequila
1/4 cup Triple Sec
1 tablespoon lime juice
1/4 cup chicken broth

Cut any excess fat from the chicken. Cut each chicken piece into
halves. Dredge the chicken with the flour; discard any excess flour.
Heat the butter in a sauté pan over medium-high heat. Add the
chicken. Cook for 2 minutes. Turn over the chicken. Add the mango,
orange and basil. Cook for about 1 minute or until the chicken is
cooked through. Remove from the heat and add the remaining
ingredients. Return to the heat. (Be careful: It may ignite if you have a
gas stove, but it will go out when the alcohol has burned off.) Cook
just enough to reduce the liquid into a coating sauce and serve.

Variations

- Try adding 1/4 cup of lime wedges for tartness.
- You can also substitute papayas for the mango (also found and
  packed the same way).
- You can add 1/4 cup sliced peeled grapefruit.
- Or try simply garnishing this dish with 1/4 cup whole raspberries.

Chicken Parmesan

pictured on page 92

2 pounds boneless skinless
   chicken breasts
1 cup flour
4 eggs, beaten
1/4 cup water
2 1/2 cups Italian-seasoned bread
   crumbs

Vegetable oil for frying
1 (16-ounce) jar spaghetti sauce
1 cup shredded mozzarella cheese
1/2 cup grated Parmesan cheese

serves 4

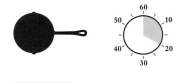

Trim any fat from the chicken. Cut the chicken pieces into halves. Dip the chicken first in the flour, then in a mixture of egg and water, then in the bread crumbs. Fry the chicken in 350-degree oil in a fryer for 10 minutes or until the pieces float and are golden brown and cooked through. If you don't have a fryer, use about 1/4 cup olive oil in a frying pan. Cook each side until golden brown. Place the fried chicken on paper towels to absorb the excess fat; then place in a baking pan. Pour the sauce over the top and cover with both cheeses. Bake in a preheated oven for 20 minutes or until the cheese has melted and is bubbly.

Variation

- Try this recipe using veal cutlets, sliced eggplant or zucchini sliced lengthwise instead of the chicken.

Chicken Cashew

pictured on page 108

serves 1

1 (8-ounce) boneless skinless chicken breast, trimmed, cut into halves
1/4 cup flour
4 tablespoons butter

1/4 cup cashews
1/4 cup diced Granny Smith apples
10 seedless grapes
1/4 cup Frangelico

Pound the chicken until thin. Dredge with the flour; discard any excess flour. Heat the butter in a sauté pan over high heat. Add the chicken. Sauté for 2 minutes. Turn over the chicken. Add the remaining ingredients except the liqueur. Cook for 2 minutes. Remove from the heat. Add the liqueur and return to the heat. (Be careful: The liqueur may ignite but the flame will die when the alcohol is burned off.) Cook for 2 minutes or until the chicken is cooked through, shaking the pan from side to side constantly.

Chicken Scampi

variation pictured on page 108

serves 2

1 pound boneless skinless chicken breasts, cut into strips
5 tablespoons flour
2 tablespoons olive oil
3 tablespoons chopped garlic

1/3 cup diced tomatoes
2 teaspoons oregano
1 teaspoon basil
1/2 teaspoon pepper
1/3 cup sliced mushrooms
1/4 cup white zinfandel

Dredge the chicken in the flour and discard the excess flour. Heat the oil over medium-high heat in a sauté pan. Sauté the chicken for 2 minutes. Add the remaining ingredients except the wine. Cook for 5 minutes or until the chicken is cooked through. Add the wine. Let the wine simmer off (about 1 minute) and serve.

Variations

- Add 1/4 cup each sliced green and red peppers.
- Try this recipe with scallops and shrimp instead of chicken.
- Add 1/4 cup more wine and 2 tablespoons butter before serving. Serve over rice or pasta.
- Try adding another 1/4 cup wine and serve over pasta.

Sun-Dried Tomato Chicken

pictured on page 108

serves 2

1 pound boneless skinless
   chicken breasts
¹/₄ cup flour
¹/₄ cup clarified butter or olive
   oil
¹/₂ cup diced tomatoes
2 tablespoons chopped sun-dried
   tomatoes (reconstituted or
   packed in oil)

¹/₄ cup diced onions
¹/₄ cup diced scallions
2 tablespoons chopped garlic
1 teaspoon oregano
1 teaspoon basil
¹/₂ cup white zinfandel
3 tablespoons grated Parmesan
   cheese

Trim any excess fat from the chicken; cut the chicken into 2-inch
strips. Dredge the chicken in the flour; discard any excess flour. Heat
the butter over medium-high heat. Add the chicken. Cook for 2
minutes and turn over the chicken. Add the remaining ingredients
except the wine and cheese. Cook for 4 minutes or until the chicken
is cooked through. Add the wine and let the wine cook off. Serve
with the cheese as a garnish.

Chicken in Vinegar Sauce

pictured on page 108

serves 4

2 tablespoons olive oil
2¹/₂ cups sliced onions
¹/₄ cup flour
2 pounds boneless skinless
   chicken breasts, cut into
   strips
¹/₂ cup white wine

¹/₂ cup chicken broth
3 tablespoons tomato paste
3 tablespoons balsamic vinegar
1¹/₂ teaspoons fresh tarragon
1 tablespoon brown sugar
¹/₂ teaspoon red pepper flakes

Heat the oil in a sauté pan over high heat. Sauté the onions in the oil
for 2 minutes. Flour the chicken strips; discard any excess flour. Add
the chicken to the sauté pan. Cook until the chicken is browned.
Combine the remaining ingredients in a bowl. Pour into the sauté
pan. Simmer, covered, over medium heat for 15 minutes or until the
chicken is cooked through. Serve immediately.

Hot Stir Fry

serves 4

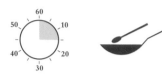

¼ cup olive oil
1 pound chicken
2 cups broccoli
½ cup sliced red peppers
1 (20-ounce) can pineapple
   chunks
2 tablespoons rice vinegar or
   white vinegar

¼ cup soy sauce
1 teaspoon garlic
2 tablespoons cornstarch
3 tablespoons green chiles
1 teaspoon red pepper flakes
1 teaspoon cilantro or coriander
1 cup bean sprouts

Heat the oil in a large sauté pan (preferably a wok) over high heat. Slice the chicken into thin strips. Place the broccoli and sliced red peppers in the pan. Stir-fry for 2 minutes. Add the chicken. Cook until the chicken has browned. Drain the juice from the canned pineapple into a bowl. Mix in the vinegar, soy sauce, garlic, cornstarch, green chiles, red pepper flakes and cilantro. Add the pineapple and bean sprouts to the sauté pan. Add the soy sauce mixture. Cook until thickened and the chicken is cooked through. Serve over rice or noodles. You may even wish to garnish it with a few sesame seeds.

Variations

- Try this with beef, pork or shrimp.
- Or use no meat at all, just the vegetables.

Carolina Fried Chicken

pictured on page 92

serves 4

2 pounds quartered chicken
   pieces
1 cup hot sauce
½ cup honey

3 cups flour
1 teaspoon pepper
Vegetable oil for frying

Place the chicken in the hot sauce and honey. Marinate in the refrigerator for 1 to 24 hours; drain well. Mix the flour and pepper in a zip-top plastic bag. Place 1 piece of chicken at a time in the bag and shake until coated. Fry in 350-degree oil in a fryer for 15 minutes or until the pieces float and are cooked through.

Curry Peaches and Chicken

serves 6

1/2 cup butter
1/2 cup diced onions
3 tablespoons chopped garlic
2 tablespoons curry powder
1 teaspoon chili powder
2 teaspoons paprika
3 pounds quartered chicken
    pieces (you can also use just
    drums or breasts)

1 cup broccoli florets
1 cup cauliflowerets
3/4 cup white wine
12 canned or fresh peach halves
1/2 cup mayonnaise
2 cups yogurt
1/2 cup shredded Monterey Jack
    cheese

Heat the butter in a sauté pan over medium heat. Sauté the onions and garlic in the butter until translucent. Add the curry powder, chili powder and paprika. Remove from the heat. Place the chicken in a shallow baking dish; coat with the sautéed mixture. Add the broccoli and cauliflower. Drizzle the wine around the chicken. Bake, covered with foil, in a preheated 375-degree oven for 30 minutes. Remove from the oven; discard the foil. Increase the oven temperature to Broil. Place the peach halves around the chicken. Mix the mayonnaise with the yogurt and spoon over the chicken, peaches and vegetables. Sprinkle with the cheese. Broil on the lower oven rack for 10 minutes or until browned and cooked through. Serve immediately.

Roast Duck a l'Orange

pictured on page 10

serves 4

1 (4-pound) mallard, cut into
    quarters
2 cups chicken stock
1 (6-ounce) jar orange marmalade
2 tablespoons dry sherry

2 tablespoons cornstarch
1 teaspoon basil
1 teaspoon thyme
2 oranges, cut into quarters
1/4 cup orange juice

Preheat the oven to 325 degrees. Place the duck on a roasting pan. Mix the remaining ingredients in a bowl and pour over the duck, allowing the excess to be caught in the drain pan. Roast in the oven for 1 hour or until cooked through, basting with the pan drippings every 10 minutes. You can thicken the sauce when it comes out of the oven by draining the juice into a saucepan and boiling it (and adding, if it needs to be thickened, a mixture of 1 teaspoon cornstarch and 2 tablespoons cold water).

Timely Tip

It's important that you always mix cornstarch with a cold ingredient before adding heat or a heated ingredient so it will mix properly and act as a thickener.

Roast Turkey

pictured on page 10

serves 15

Perfect Gravy

1 to 2 cups chicken stock
1 teaspoon chopped garlic
1 teaspoon basil
1 teaspoon oregano
1 tablespoon Gravy Master or liquid
    seasoning
1 teaspoon black pepper
1 cup butter (2 sticks)
1/3 cup flour
2 tablespoons sour cream

Remove as much fat as you can from the pan drippings (the fat is the clear juice in the drippings). Place the roasting pan with rack on the stove over medium heat. Add the chicken stock, stirring to incorporate all the browned bits. Add the garlic, basil, oregano, Gravy Master and pepper. Melt the butter in a saucepan. Add the flour to the butter and mix well. Add to the stock mixture. Cook for 10 minutes or until thickened, stirring constantly. Stir in the sour cream just before serving.

1 (18-pound) whole turkey
3 tablespoons soy sauce
2 tablespoons honey

pinch (less than a quarter
    teaspoon) of pepper

Stuff the cavity of the turkey if you wish. (Remember that over-stuffing the cavity may lead to soggy and sticky stuffing, and may even split the breast as it roasts). Preheat the oven to 350 degrees. Place the turkey in a roasting pan. Mix the remaining ingredients in a bowl. Brush all the mixture over the turkey. Roast for about 4 hours or until a meat thermometer registers 175 degrees (remember to test the temperature in the thickest part of the thigh, not touching any bone). Another sign of doneness is that inserting a pronged fork into the thigh produces clear juices. Also, the turkey should be uncovered during the first 30 minutes of cooking; then remove from the oven, baste with pan drippings and place a piece of foil loosely over the top of the turkey (to prevent burning). Continue cooking, repeating the basting every 30 minutes. For the last hour of cooking, remove the foil to allow the turkey to brown further. If the turkey looks like it's going to burn, simply put the foil back on. When the turkey is done, remove it to a platter and allow it to cool for at least 20 minutes before carving it.

Variation

- Turkey may also be cooked using another method, at a lower temperature of 325 degrees. In this type of roasting, the turkey is basted every 45 minutes, remains uncovered and is rotated from breast side down to leg side down. The biggest problem with this method is that it takes practice to gracefully turn the turkey as it cooks, but the reward to this technique is that it browns the fat on the turkey evenly and produces great drippings for gravy.

Basic Stuffing

1 cup diced onion
1 cup diced celery
1/2 cup butter
1 tablespoon chopped garlic
1 teaspoon pepper
1 tablespoon oregano
1 teaspoon celery salt

2 tablespoons poultry seasoning
　　mix or sage
6 cups crumb stuffing mix, or
　　8 cups cubed stale bread
2 eggs
1 1/4 cups chicken stock

stuffing for an 8-pound turkey
or chicken

Sauté the onion and celery in a sauté pan over medium-high heat for about 5 minutes. Mix with the remaining ingredients in a bowl. You can stuff the bird with this, or you can bake it separately in a casserole dish, adding another cup of chicken stock. Bake, covered with foil, at 350 degrees for at least 45 minutes or until done.

Variations

- To make **Corn Bread Stuffing,** replace the bread crumbs with crumbled corn bread and add 1 cup frozen corn.
- To make **Chestnut Stuffing,** add 1 cup chopped chestnuts or chestnut purée and 1 tablespoon thyme. (To get the meat out of the chestnut, cut a gash in the flat side of the chestnut and boil in water for 5 minutes. Drain the water and peel off the shell.)
- To make **Sausage Stuffing,** simply brown about 1/2 pound loose sausage. Add to any of the variations or leave it by itself.
- To make **Jalapeño Stuffing,** add 1/2 cup chopped chiles to the sautéing process; add 2 cups shredded jalapeño Monterey Jack cheese, 2 tablespoons Tabasco sauce or hot sauce, 2 tablespoons cilantro and 1/2 cup salsa to the mixing process. This is also a great addition to the Corn Bread Stuffing variation.

Basic Barbecue Sauce

makes 3 cups

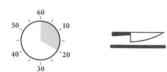

2 cups catsup
3/4 cup cider vinegar
1/4 cup packed brown sugar

3 tablespoons Worcestershire
   sauce

Mix all the ingredients together. Remember that this is just a base;
unless you add a variation, it will be bland and very tomato-y.

Variations

- Add to the base 1 cup beer, 2 tablespoons chopped garlic,
  1 tablespoon hot sauce and 2 tablespoons oregano.
- For a fruity twist, add to the base 1 cup chopped mango,
  2 tablespoons basil and 1/2 cup apricot jam.
- For **Honey Mustard Barbecue Sauce,** add to the base 1/2 cup
  honey and 1/2 cup Dijon mustard.
- Add your favorite flavor combinations to the base to make your
  own sauce.

Kick-Your-Butt Barbecue Sauce

pictured on page 10

makes 7 cups

2 tablespoons olive oil
1/4 cup chopped garlic
4 cups diced onions
1/4 cup diced green chiles
1/4 cup chopped jalapeños
2 cups catsup
1 cup Worcestershire sauce

2/3 cup packed brown sugar
1/2 cup cider vinegar
1/2 cup lemon juice
1/4 cup chili powder
2 tablespoons Grey Poupon
   mustard or a grainy mustard
2 tablespoons oregano

Heat the oil in a saucepan. Add the garlic, onions, chiles and
jalapeños. Cook over medium heat for 3 minutes. Add the remaining
ingredients. Simmer for 20 minutes. Let cool before using. Store in the
refrigerator. This sauce may also be used on all seafood, poultry, pork,
beef and vegetables being cooked on the grill.

Honey-Mustard Marinade

1 cup mustard (preferably Grey Poupon)

1/2 cup honey
1/4 cup olive oil

makes 2 cups

Mix it all together and use as a marinade as desired.

Herb and Spice Marinade

1 cup olive oil
1 tablespoon basil
1 tablespoon oregano
1 tablespoon thyme
1 tablespoon chopped garlic

1 teaspoon pepper
1 bay leaf
1/4 cup balsamic vinegar
1 tablespoon honey

makes 2 cups

Mix it all together and use as a marinade as desired.

Texas Grilling Rub

1/2 cup paprika
1/4 cup black pepper
1/4 cup chili powder
1/4 cup sugar

3 tablespoons salt
2 tablespoons garlic powder
1 tablespoon ground cayenne

makes 2 cups

Mix all the ingredients together and store in a refrigerator.

Timely Tip

This can be rubbed on things grilled or roasted or on things like seafood, beef, pork or chicken. Use enough to coat the food; the more you use, the more flavorful it will be.

Seafood & Meatless Entrées

Boiled Lobster

pictured on page 56

2 quarts water   1 (1½-pound) lobster   *serves 1*

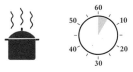

Bring the water to a boil. Plunge the lobster head first into the water. Boil, covered, for 12 minutes; drain well. Serve with melted butter. The lobster should be fully immersed in liquid the whole time it is cooking. When done, it should be reddish in color and the tail of the lobster should spring back when opened.

Variation

- For a different flavor, use one of the butters from page 148.

Broiled Scallops with Capers and Sweet Peppers

2 pounds sea scallops or   1 tablespoon chopped garlic   *serves 6*
   bay scallops   ¼ cup white wine
1 tablespoon olive oil   ½ cup bread crumbs
¾ cup finely diced green   ¼ cup capers, drained
   peppers   1 teaspoon dill weed
¾ cup finely diced red peppers   ¼ cup butter

Preheat the oven to 500 degrees. Arrange the scallops in a single layer in a baking dish. Heat the oil in a sauté pan over medium heat. Sauté the peppers and garlic in the oil just until the peppers are wilted. Mix in the wine, bread crumbs, capers and dillweed. Spread over the scallops. Dot with the butter. Broil for about 6 minutes. Serve immediately.

Seared Sea Scallops and Pasta with Pesto

serves 2

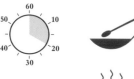

1/2 cup chopped fresh parsley
1/4 cup finely chopped pistachios
1 teaspoon grated lemon peel
1/4 teaspoon cumin
1/4 teaspoon pepper
2 tablespoons fresh lemon juice

1 tablespoon olive oil
1/4 cup flour
3/4 pound sea scallops
1/4 cup butter
1/2 pound pasta, cooked
   (preferably angel hair)

Process the parsley, pistachios, lemon peel, cumin, pepper, lemon juice and olive oil in a food processor until smooth. Set aside. Place the flour and scallops in a zip-top plastic bag and shake until coated. Place sauté pan over high heat for 1 minute. Add the butter to the pan and let melt. Remove the scallops from plastic bag 1 at a time and place in the butter. Cook for 4 minutes per side. Add the hot pasta to the pesto mix and toss. Divide evenly on 2 plates. Top with the scallops. Serve immediately.

Variations

- Try this with 3/4 pound thinly sliced boneless chicken breasts.
- It's also exceptional prepared with peeled deveined shrimp.
- This is even great just plain, without scallops.

Scallops Nantucket

serves 4

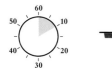

1 1/2 pounds scallops, oysters or
   lobster meat
3/4 cup dry vermouth
1/4 cup bread crumbs

1/4 cup butter
3/4 cup shredded mozzarella
   cheese
1 tablespoon parsley

Preheat the oven to 375 degrees. Place the scallops in a shallow casserole. Top with the vermouth and bread crumbs. Top the crumbs with the butter. Bake for about 15 minutes. Remove from the oven and top with the cheese and parsley. Return to the oven. Cook for 10 minutes or until the cheese has melted and is bubbling.

Baked Stuffed Shrimp

serves 4

1/4 cup butter
1/2 cup finely chopped onion
1/4 cup finely chopped celery
1 teaspoon chopped garlic
1 teaspoon oregano
1 teaspoon basil

1 teaspoon dill
1 3/4 cups crushed Ritz crackers
1 egg
12 shrimp (size U12)
1/2 cup white wine

Melt the butter in a sauté pan over medium heat. Add the onion, celery, garlic, oregano, basil and dill. Sauté for 5 minutes and pour into a bowl. Add the cracker crumbs and mix well. Add the egg. Peel the shrimp except for the tails. Split the shrimp with a paring knife up the center without actually cutting them in half. Stuff each shrimp with stuffing the size of a golf ball. Poke the tail into the stuffing to almost cover it. Placc in a greased baking dish. Bake in a preheated 375-degree oven for 20 minutes. Serve with drawn butter and fresh lemon wedges.

Variations

- Add 1 cup chopped scallops during the sautéing process for scallop stuffing.
- Add 1 cup crab meat for crab stuffing.
- Try this stuffing for fish.
- Top a large fish fillet with stuffing and bake.
- It's also great baked on top of scallops.

Oops . . . Oops . . . Oops . . . Oops . . .

If you're having trouble rolling the stuffing into a ball, it may not be moist enough, so just add a little more butter. Stuffing should be just moist enough to hold together. If it's too moist, add more Ritz cracker crumbs to it. Overcooked shrimp will be tough and dried out, so if this happens, cook it at a lower temperature or remove it from the oven earlier.

Batter-Fried Shrimp

serves 6

2 pounds uncooked shrimp
3/4 cup flour
1/2 cup water
1/4 cup beer (if you don't want to add beer, add more water)

1 egg
1 tablespoon sugar
1/2 teaspoon salt
Vegetable oil for frying

Peel and devein the shrimp, leaving the tails on. Cut the shrimp from the bottom about halfway up (better known as butterflying shrimp). Mix the next 6 ingredients together. Dip the shrimp into the batter. Fry in 375-degree oil until golden brown (about 3 minutes, depending on the size of the shrimp). Drain on a paper towel. Serve by itself or with cocktail or tartar sauce.

Variation

•   Try this recipe with fillet of sole, trout or bass.

Hot and Spicy Shrimp

variation pictured on page 108

2 tablespoons olive oil
¹/₄ cup flour
³/₄ pound deveined peeled
    shrimp
¹/₂ cup finely diced broccoli
    florets
1 teaspoon chopped garlic
¹/₄ cup diced onions
¹/₄ cup diced red peppers
¹/₄ cup diced scallions

¹/₄ cup sliced mushrooms
1 teaspoon oregano
1 teaspoon basil
1 teaspoon crushed red pepper
    flakes
1 tablespoon brown sugar
¹/₄ cup soy sauce
¹/₄ cup chicken broth or orange
    juice

serves 2

Heat the oil in a sauté pan over high heat. Flour the shrimp,
discarding any excess flour. Place the shrimp in the sauté pan.
Add the broccoli, garlic, onions, red peppers, scallions, mushrooms,
oregano, basil and red pepper flakes. Sauté for 4 minutes. Add the
remaining ingredients and cook for 3 to 4 minutes. If you want the
sauce to be a little thicker, add a little flour during cooking (about 1
teaspoon). Serve alone or over rice.

Variations

- Try this with scallops, boneless chicken, sliced beef, veal or pork.
- Surprisingly enough, this is quite good if you omit the shrimp and
  add more vegetables. Try ¹/₂ cup chopped green pepper and ³/₄
  cup diced eggplant.

Seafood Fra Diablo

serves 2

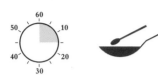

2 tablespoons olive oil
6 shrimp, peeled, sliced down
   the center
$1/2$ cup scallops
6 closed littlenecks, washed
$1^1/2$ cups spaghetti sauce

1 teaspoon red pepper
$1/2$ teaspoon basil
$1/2$ teaspoon oregano
$3/4$ pound pasta of your choice,
   cooked

Heat the oil in a sauté pan over high heat. Add the seafood, tossing as it cooks. Sauté for 2 minutes. Add the next 4 ingredients. Cook for 5 minutes. Serve over the pasta. Pry the clam shells open with a knife if needed.

Variations

- Omit all the seafood and add $1/2$ cup sliced chourico and one 8-ounce boneless skinless chicken breast cut into strips.
- Omit all the listed seafood and add 12 cleaned mussels.
- Try it with only shrimp or scallops.
- Even better, try it over rice.

Spicy Fried Squid

2 pounds squid, cleaned (about 4 cups sliced) (buy it cleaned—you can also buy it already sliced at your fish market)

1/2 cup buttermilk

1 tablespoon Tabasco sauce

1/4 cup Cajun seasoning

3 cups clam fry mix (you can also find this at the fish market)

Vegetable oil for frying

serves 6

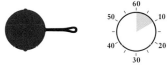

If you didn't buy it sliced, cut the squid into 1/8-inch slices; cut the tentacles into bite-size pieces. Place the squid in a bowl. Add the buttermilk, Tabasco sauce and Cajun seasoning. Marinate for about 5 minutes; drain as well as you can. Coat the squid in small batches in the clam fry mix. Fry in 350-degree oil until they are golden brown in color (about 1 minute). Don't overcook, or the squid will be like rubber. Serve with cocktail sauce and banana pepper rings, or with lemon wedges and tartar sauce.

Variations

- Try this with scallops, clams, oysters, shrimp and small fillets of fish. Cook just until golden in color.
- If you don't want it spicy, don't add the Cajun seasoning and Tabasco sauce. It can be done plain as well, or try it with 1 teaspoon dill instead of the seasoning.

Roasted Fillet of Fish

pictured on page 10

serves 8

1 (5-pound) fillet of fish,
   preferably with skin on 1 side
   (bass, grouper, halibut or any
   flake-style fish)
3 tablespoons olive oil
¹/₂ cup finely diced red peppers
¹/₂ cup finely diced onions

2 tablespoons minced garlic
1 tablespoon oregano
1 tablespoon basil
1 tablespoon dill
1 tablespoon parsley
1 tablespoon paprika

Place the fish skin side down on a roasting rack. Brush the top with the oil. Sprinkle each ingredient over the fillet. (You can actually use any size fish you choose; just make sure that you have enough of the seasonings to cover the top of the fillet.) Roast in a preheated 400-degree oven until the fish becomes flaky. Remember when roasting to keep your rack close to the top of the oven. For a 5-pound fillet, allow to roast at least 30 minutes. You can check doneness by looking at the center of the fish and lifting a flake apart with a fork. If it's white and flakes apart easily, it's done; if it's translucent and doesn't flake apart easily, it still needs a little more time in the oven.

Sole Piccata

variation pictured on page 108

3 tablespoons olive oil or butter
2 eggs
1/4 cup flour
2 (3-ounce) boneless skinless
    fillets of sole

1 tablespoon capers, drained
1/4 lemon

serves 1

Heat the oil in a sauté pan over high heat. Beat the eggs in a bowl and set aside. Flour the fish and dip in the egg batter, coating the whole fillet. Place quickly into the sauté pan. Cook for 1 minute or until golden brown on 1 side; turn the fillet over. Add the capers and squeeze the juice from the lemon into the pan. Cook until browned on both sides. This dish cooks really fast, so don't take your eyes off it.

Variation

- Try this with sliced boneless chicken or veal.

Oops . . . Oops . . . Oops . . . Oops . . .

If your egg batter is not crisping and browning (or doesn't even seem to be cooking), then your oil is not hot enough.

Grilled Swordfish Fillets with Lemon Dill Butter

pictured on page 10

serves 1

1 swordfish fillet, 1 inch
   thick

1 tablespoon mayonnaise or
   olive oil

This can either be done on a hot grill outside or in the oven on broil. Brush the fillet with the mayonnaise to keep it from sticking to the grill; if you're broiling, just spray a little nonstick cooking spray on the pan. Cook for about 3 minutes per side or until the fish is firm to the touch and fork tender. Serve with a pat of Lemon Dill Butter or alone.

Lemon Dill Butter

makes ¹/₂ cup

2 sticks butter, softened
1 tablespoon lemon juice

1 tablespoon grated lemon peel
1 tablespoon dill

Mix all the ingredients in a bowl. Serve a dollop on the fish. You can also roll the butter in waxed paper like a cigar, and cut round ¹/₄-inch slices onto the fish.

Variations

- This butter is great on grilled steaks and other kinds of fish such as salmon, tuna, trout and bass.
- Make **Sun-Dried Tomato Butter** by mixing the butter, ¹/₄ cup chopped sun-dried tomatoes and 1 tablespoon basil.
- Make **Citrus Butter** by mixing the butter, 1 tablespoon lemon juice, 1 tablespoon orange juice, 2 tablespoons grated orange peel, 1 tablespoon grated lemon peel and 2 tablespoons grated lime peel.
- To make **Red Hot Garlic Butter,** mix the butter, 1 tablespoon ground red pepper, 2 tablespoons chopped garlic and 1 tablespoon chopped parsley.
- This is really easy to do and adds a great flavor. Try your own variations.

Orzo Twist

3/4 cup uncooked orzo pasta
1 tablespoon olive oil
1/2 cup chopped sweet onion
2 tablespoons chopped garlic
1/2 cup oil-pack sun-dried
    tomatoes, finely chopped
1/4 cup pine nuts

1/3 cup chopped fresh basil
    (about 15 leaves)
1 tablespoon Tabasco sauce (or
    your favorite hot sauce)
1 cup half-and-half
1/3 cup grated Romano cheese
1/4 cup crumbled goat cheese

serves 4

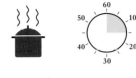

Cook the pasta as directed on the package. Heat the oil in a sauté pan over medium heat. Sauté the onion, garlic, tomatoes, pine nuts and basil in the oil for 5 to 8 minutes or until the onion becomes translucent. Add the Tabasco sauce and half-and-half. Simmer for about 5 minutes (until it's thickened a little). Add the Romano cheese. Simmer for 2 minutes or until the cheese melts. Stir in the pasta. Garnish with the goat cheese and serve.

Sassy Sweet-and-Sour Veggie Pasta

1 pound thin spaghetti
2 tablespoons butter
1/2 cup diced red peppers
1/2 cup sliced onions
1/2 cup sliced mushrooms
1/2 cup grated carrots
2 tablespoons chopped garlic
1 1/2 cups broccoli florets

1 tablespoon oregano
1 teaspoon basil
1 tablespoon red pepper flakes
1 tablespoon brown sugar
3 tablespoons cider vinegar
1/4 cup soy sauce
1/4 cup white wine
2 tablespoons honey

serves 4

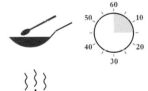

Cook the pasta as directed on the package. Melt the butter in a sauté pan over medium-high heat. Sauté the red peppers, onions, mushrooms, carrots, garlic, broccoli, oregano, basil and red pepper flakes in the butter for about 8 minutes. Add the remaining ingredients and bring to a boil. Pour into a large bowl. Add the pasta and mix well.

Basic Quiche

serves 4

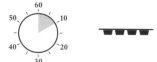

4 eggs, beaten

2 cups half-and-half or light cream

pinch of salt, pepper and nutmeg

1 ready-made pie pastry

Mix the eggs, half-and-half and seasonings in a bowl. Pour the mixture into a pie plate lined with the pie pastry. Bake in a preheated 350-degree oven for 45 minutes.

Variations

- For **Bacon and Cheese Quiche,** mix in 2 cups shredded Swiss or Cheddar cheese and $1/2$ pound crumbled cooked bacon. Cook as directed.
- For **Spinach Quiche,** mix in $1/2$ cup chopped spinach and 1 table-spoon chopped fresh basil.
- For **Broccoli and Cheese Quiche,** mix in 1 cup shredded Cheddar cheese and $1/2$ cup chopped broccoli.
- For **Ham and Mushroom Quiche,** mix in $1/2$ cup sliced mushrooms, $1/2$ cup diced ham and $1/4$ cup chopped onion.
- For **Crab Quiche,** mix in 1 cup chopped crab meat.
- Your mixtures can be just about anything. To retain texture I try not to mix in more than $2^1/2$ cups of extra ingredients.

Mari's Southern Tomato Pie

2 ready-made pie pastries	1/2 cup mayonnaise	*serves 4*
3 cups diced tomatoes	2 tablespoons basil	
3/4 cup diced onions	1 teaspoon pepper	
2 cups shredded white Cheddar cheese		

Fit 1 pie pastry into a greased pie plate. Preheat the oven to 350 degrees. Mix the tomatoes, onions, cheese, mayonnaise, basil and pepper together. Pour into the prepared pie plate. Top with the remaining pie pastry, sealing the edge together by pinching. Bake for 1 hour. Let cool for 15 minutes before serving.

Cocktail Sauce

pictured on page 154

3/4 cup catsup	3 tablespoons horseradish	*makes 1 cup*
1/4 cup honey	2 tablespoons chili sauce	
3 tablespoons lemon juice		

Mix all the ingredients together and serve.

Tartar Sauce

3/4 cup mayonnaise	3 tablespoons lemon juice	*makes 1 cup*
1/4 cup pickle relish		

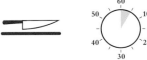

Mix all the ingredients in a bowl and serve.

Cran-Orange Marinade

makes 2¹/₂ cups

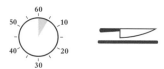

1 cup cranberry jelly
¹/₂ cup orange juice
2 tablespoons honey

2 tablespoons Dijon mustard
1 cup orange wedges

Mix it all together and use as a marinade as desired.

Pesto Marinade

makes 2 cups

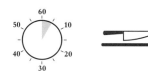

1 cup olive oil
¹/₃ cup chopped fresh parsley
¹/₃ cup chopped fresh basil

2 tablespoons chopped garlic
¹/₃ cup pineapple juice

Mix it all together and use as a marinade as desired.

Lemon Pepper Marinade

makes 1³/₄ cups

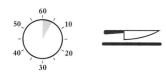

1 cup olive oil
¹/₂ cup lemon wedges
1 teaspoon basil

2 teaspoons pepper
3 tablespoons lemon juice
1 tablespoon honey

Mix it all together and use as a marinade as desired.

Thai Marinade

1/2 cup soy sauce
1/4 cup cider vinegar
1/4 cup diced green chiles
1 teaspoon black pepper

1 teaspoon red pepper
2 tablespoons chopped jalapeños
1/4 cup orange juice
1 teaspoon tamari

makes 1 1/2 cups

Mix it all together and use as a marinade as desired.

Yogurt Mint Marinade

1/4 cup chopped fresh parsley
1/2 cup chopped fresh mint
1/4 cup chopped scallions
1/2 cup lemon juice

1 cup plain yogurt
1 teaspoon Dijon mustard
1 teaspoon pepper

makes 2 1/2 cups

Mix it all together and use as a marinade as desired.

Timely Tip

If you want to use a leftover marinade as a dipping sauce, you must first boil it for 5 minutes to kill any harmful bacteria from the uncooked meat or poultry.

Desserts

Desserts

Pictured on overleaf (recipe page numbers can be found in the index):

Dixie Bourbon Balls, Linzer Torte, Coconut Macaroons, Peanut Butter Cookies, Chocolate-Kissed Peanut Butter Cookies, Mari's Southern Tomato Pie, Mushroom Quiche (a variation of Basic Quiche), Sweet Potato Pie, Oatmeal Cookies, Almond Dreams, Chocolate Candy Clusters, Oatmeal Pie

Inset photos (left to right): Spanish Rice with Black Beans, Chocolate Cream Pie; Perfect Baked Potato, Ginger Broccoli, Calzone, Super Easy Cheesecake; Whiskey Cake

All these dishes were prepared using the Baking, Cold Cookery, and Boiling techniques.

Basic White Cake

2½ cups flour
1½ cups sugar
3 tablespoons baking powder
1 teaspoon salt

½ cup shortening, oil or butter
1 cup milk
1 teaspoon vanilla extract
2 eggs

serves 8

Mix all the ingredients with an electric mixer until smooth. Don't overmix; it should only take at the longest 5 minutes. Bake in a greased springform pan in a preheated 350-degree oven for 30 minutes or until a wooden pick inserted in the center comes out clean. Let cool and choose a frosting or eat it plain.

Variations

- Mix in ¾ cup cocoa powder and 1 more tablespoon baking powder for **Chocolate Cake.**
- Mix in 2 more tablespoons vanilla extract for **Vanilla Cake.**
- Mix in ½ cup strawberry jam, 1 tablespoon strawberry extract and 1 more tablespoon baking powder for **Strawberry Cake.**
- Mix in ½ cup peanut butter, ½ cup peanut butter chips and 1 more tablespoon baking powder for **Peanut Butter Cake.**

Oops . . . Oops . . . Oops . . . Oops . . .

If the top of your cake has sunk to the bottom of the pan, one of three things may have happened: You may have taken the cake out before it had finished rising; you may have slammed the oven door; or you added baking soda and not baking powder. These two totally different ingredients have opposite effects.

Chocolate Layer Cake

pictured on page 136

serves 10

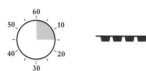

Timely Tip

Something everyone needs to know about frosting is that the butter and shortening are interchangeable. However, we generally use butter in cooler temperatures and shortening in hotter temperatures because butter melts and shortening holds up better at higher temperatures. Another tip: If the frosting is tearing the cake beneath it, try adding a tablespoon of water to the frosting to help make it smoother and easier to spread.

2 cups flour
1 1/2 cups sugar
3/4 cup baking cocoa
1 teaspoon salt
2 teaspoons baking powder
1/4 teaspoon baking soda
2 eggs
1 tablespoon vanilla extract
1/2 cup vegetable oil
1 cup milk
1/2 cup water
1/2 cup chocolate morsels
Chocolate Frosting

Preheat the oven to 350 degrees. Butter a 9-inch round layer pan or spray with a nonstick spray like Pam. Mix the first 6 ingredients in a large bowl, spooning out any lumps that may appear. Add the eggs, vanilla, oil and milk in the order given, stirring constantly. Bring the water to a boil in a saucepan. Turn off the heat and add the chocolate morsels. Stir until almost melted together and add to the batter. Mix until smooth, preferably with an electric hand mixer for about 5 minutes. Don't worry if all the chocolate hasn't melted. Pour into the prepared pan. Bake for 30 to 35 minutes. Let cool for 10 minutes. Invert onto a wire rack. Cool completely. Spread Chocolate Frosting between the layers and over the top and side of the cake.

Chocolate Frosting

makes 2 cups

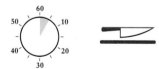

3 3/4 cups confectioners' sugar
1/2 cup baking cocoa
1/2 cup butter
1 tablespoon vanilla extract
1/3 cup milk

Mix all the ingredients together using an electric mixer. Beat at high speed for 2 minutes.

Chocolate Macaroon Tunnel Cake

1¹/₄ cups sugar
5 tablespoons olive oil
2 eggs
1¹/₄ teaspoons baking soda
2 tablespoons vanilla extract
¹/₂ teaspoon salt
1¹/₂ cups buttermilk

3 cups flour
¹/₂ cup sweetened flaked
    coconut
¹/₂ cup baking cocoa
³/₄ cup confectioners' sugar
1¹/₄ tablespoons water

serves 10

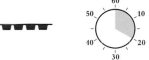

Preheat the oven to 350 degrees. Using an electric mixer, combine the sugar and oil in a large bowl. Mix in 1 egg at a time. Add the baking soda, vanilla, salt, buttermilk and flour. Remove 1 cup of the batter and mix with the coconut in a separate bowl. Add the cocoa to the other batter. Pour half the cocoa batter into a bundt pan sprayed with nonstick spray. Spoon the coconut batter into the center of the cocoa batter to form a ring, being careful not to touch the sides. Cover the coconut ring with the remaining cocoa batter. Bake for 40 minutes or until a wooden pick inserted into the center comes out clean. Let cool for 10 minutes before removing from the pan. Combine the confectioners' sugar and water in a small bowl and drizzle over the cooled cake.

Oops . . . Oops . . . Oops . . . Oops . . .

"Oh, no! My coconut ring is touching the side!" Don't worry, you didn't ruin the cake. Keeping the ring in the center of the cake allows the white to be totally covered. If the coconut mixture touches the sides then the cake, when done, will simply not be a uniform color on the outside.

Old-Fashioned Pound Cake

serves 10

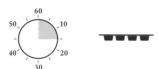

3 cups flour
1/4 teaspoon salt
1/4 teaspoon baking soda
2 sticks butter (1 cup)

3 cups sugar
6 large egg yolks
1 cup sour cream
6 large egg whites

Mix the flour, salt, baking soda, butter and sugar together. Add the egg yolks 1 at a time. Mix in the sour cream. Beat the egg whites until stiff and fold into the batter with a spoon (do not use an electric mixer at this stage). Pour into a greased fluted tube pan or a springform pan (the fluted pan just gives it a better appearance). Bake in a preheated 300-degree oven for 1 1/2 hours or until a wooden pick inserted in the center comes out clean.

Whiskey or Rum Cake

pictured on page 56

serves 8

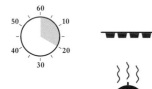

1 Basic White Cake
   (page 157)
1/2 cup water

3/4 cup spice rum or premium
   whiskey
1 cup sugar

Prepare and bake the cake. Mix the water, rum and sugar in a saucepan. Boil for 5 minutes. Let cool for 10 minutes. Pour over the hot cake; the cake will absorb the liquid better if you make a hole in the cake with a skewer. This cake needs no frosting; however, it's okay if you drizzle a mixture of 1/2 cup confectioners' sugar and 3 tablespoons water over the top (more for appearance than taste).

Blueberry Crumb Muffins

pictured on page 136

1/4 cup butter
3/4 cup sugar
2 cups flour
2 1/2 teaspoons baking powder
1/2 teaspoon salt
2 eggs
1/2 cup milk

1 tablespoon honey
2 cups blueberries
1/2 cup sugar
1/3 cup flour
1 teaspoon cinnamon
1/4 cup butter, softened

makes 6 muffins

Combine 1/4 cup butter and 3/4 cup sugar in a large bowl. Mix together with an electric hand mixer on medium speed. Add in 2 cups flour, baking powder, salt, eggs, milk and honey; the batter should be rather thick. Mix the blueberries into the batter with a spoon. Butter or spray muffin tins. Fill each almost to the top with batter. Mix 1/2 cup sugar, 1/3 cup flour, cinnamon and 1/4 cup butter until crumbly. Sprinkle over the muffins. Bake in a preheated 325-degree oven for 30 to 35 minutes or until a wooden pick inserted in the center of a muffin comes out clean.

Variations

- To make **Apple Muffins,** replace the blueberries with 1 cup diced peeled Granny Smith apples. Add 1 cup applesauce and 1 teaspoon cinnamon, then continue with the directions.
- To make **Cranberry Nut Muffins,** replace the blueberries with 1 1/2 cups cranberries and 1/2 cup chopped walnuts. Continue with the directions.
- To make **Raspberry Muffins,** replace the blueberries with 2 cups raspberries and continue with the directions.
- This recipe can also be done without the crumb topping.
- Try baking this batter in a loaf pan for a quick bread.

Mocha Frosting

makes enough for 1 cake

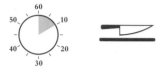

1 teaspoon instant coffee
$^1/_4$ cup milk
$^1/_3$ cup butter or shortening,
    softened

1 pound confectioners' sugar

Mix with an electric mixer until smooth. You may want to add a little more milk to help with the consistency for good spreading.

Cream Cheese Frosting

makes enough for 1 cake

8 ounces cream cheese, softened
1 tablespoon milk

1 teaspoon vanilla
$5^1/_2$ cups confectioners' sugar

Mix all the ingredients until smooth.

Variations

- Try mixing in $^1/_3$ cup crushed peppermint candy for **Creamy Peppermint Frosting.**
- Mix in 1 tablespoon almond extract for **Almond Cream Cheese Frosting.**

Butter Cream Frosting

makes enough for 1 cake

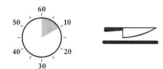

$^1/_2$ cup butter, softened
1 pound confectioners' sugar

1 tablespoon vanilla extract
3 tablespoons milk

Mix the butter and confectioners' sugar first. Add the vanilla and milk 1 at a time, mixing well after each addition.

Cocoa Peppermint Frosting

1/2 cup butter, softened
1/2 cup baking cocoa
32/3 cups confectioners' sugar

7 tablespoons milk
1 tablespoon crushed
   peppermint candy

makes enough for 1 cake

Mix the butter, cocoa, confectioners' sugar and milk until smooth. Stir in the candy.

Coconut Frosting

1/2 cup butter, softened
1 cup packed brown sugar
1/4 cup milk

2 cups confectioners' sugar
1 cup flaked coconut

makes enough for 1 cake

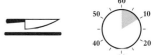

Mix the butter, brown sugar, milk and confectioners' sugar until smooth. Stir in the coconut.

Peanut Butter Frosting

1/4 cup butter, softened
1/4 cup peanut butter
1 teaspoon vanilla extract

21/2 cups confectioners' sugar
1/4 cup milk

makes enough for 1 cake

Mix all the ingredients together until smooth.

Timely Tip

If your frosting mixture is too stiff, add milk or water 1 tablespoon at a time to obtain the desired consistency. If it is too loose, gradually add more confectioners' sugar.

Chocolate Candy Clusters

pictured on page 154

serves 6, twelve clusters

6 ounces semisweet chocolate
    morsels
1 tablespoon shortening

3/4 cup dry-roasted peanuts
    (not salted)

Melt the chocolate morsels and shortening in a double boiler over simmering (not boiling) water. Remove from the heat and add the peanuts. Let cool for 1 to 2 minutes. Drop spoonfuls of the mixture onto waxed paper. Let cool for 1 hour in the refrigerator before eating.

Variations

- Use 1/2 cup nuts and add 1/3 cup raisins for **Raisin Nut Clusters.**
- Add to the chocolate 1/2 cup crisp rice cereal and 1/2 cup broken-up caramel for **Caramel Clusters.**
- Add 1/4 cup peanut butter to the mixture for **Peanut Butter Clusters.**

Fudge Squares

serves 10

18 ounces semisweet chocolate
    morsels
1 (14-ounce) can sweetened
    condensed milk

1 teaspoon vanilla extract
1 cup chopped pecans or
    walnuts

Butter an 8x8x2-inch glass baking dish. Place the chocolate morsels in a double boiler over hot, not boiling, water. Melt the chocolate, stirring constantly. Remove from the heat and stir in the remaining ingredients in the order given. Spread the mixture in the buttered dish. Let cool for at least 3 hours before cutting into squares.

Variations

- Substitute 3/4 cup crunchy-style peanut butter for the nuts for a **Chocolate Peanut Butter Fudge.**
- Fold in 1/2 cup miniature marshmallows for **Rocky Road Fudge.**
- Layer the bottom of the buttered dish with crushed graham crackers. Replace the nuts with miniature marshmallows. Spread the fudge mixture over the graham crackers for **S'mores Fudge.**

Timely Tip

Double boiling is easy: Bring a saucepan 1/4 full of water to a simmer. Place the food (in this case chocolate morsels) in a bowl over the saucepan. The steam will heat the bottom of the bowl and melt the chocolate. The chocolate will only melt properly if stirred constantly during this process and if the water is at a slow simmer. Boiling water tends to burn the chocolate.

Super Easy Cheesecake

pictured on page 178

serves 8

1½ cups graham cracker crumbs
2 tablespoons sugar
6 tablespoons melted butter
32 ounces cream cheese,
  softened
1½ cups sugar
6 egg yolks

¼ teaspoon salt
1 tablespoon flour
1 tablespoon cornstarch
2 tablespoons vanilla extract
2 tablespoons lemon juice
2 cups sour cream
6 large egg whites

Preheat the oven to 325 degrees. Assemble and grease a 10-inch springform pan. Mix the first 3 ingredients together and press into the prepared pan (this is the crust). Beat the cream cheese in a mixing bowl with an electric mixer until fluffy. Add 1½ cups sugar gradually, stirring constantly. Beat in egg yolks 1 at a time. Blend in (in this order) the salt, flour, cornstarch, vanilla, lemon juice and sour cream. Whip the egg whites in a separate bowl until soft peaks form. Fold the egg whites into the cream cheese mixture with a spoon, mixing just enough to blend. Pour the batter into the pan. Bake for 1 hour. Turn off the oven and let the cheesecake stand in the closed oven for 1 hour. Remove from the oven and chill in the refrigerator for 2 hours before serving.

Variations

- Add some fruit on the top as a garnish.
- To make **Marble Cheesecake,** pour half the batter in the springform pan. Add 1 cup melted semisweet chocolate to the remaining batter and pour into the pan. Swirl the batter with a knife. Then continue baking as directed above.
- To make **Pumpkin Cheesecake,** add ¾ cup packed pumpkin to the batter with 1 tablespoon cinnamon and 1 teaspoon nutmeg.

Chocolate Chip Cookies

pictured on page 136

makes 15 cookies

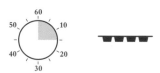

3/4 cup sugar
3/4 cup packed brown sugar
1 cup butter, softened
2 eggs, beaten
2 1/4 cups flour

1 teaspoon baking soda
1 teaspoon salt
1 tablespoon vanilla extract
1 (12-ounce) package semisweet
 chocolate morsels

Cream the sugars and butter in a mixer bowl. Add the eggs. Mix in the remaining ingredients except the chocolate morsels until smooth. Add the chocolate morsels. Drop rounded spoonfuls of the mixture 2 inches apart onto a buttered cookie sheet. Bake in a preheated oven at 350 degrees for 12 minutes or until golden brown.

Variations

- Simply add 1/2 cup chopped nuts for **Nutty Chocolate Chip Cookies.**
- Mix in 1/2 cup white chocolate chunks for **Chocolate Delight.**
- Try cooking the mixture in a pie dish and serve sliced as a pie.

Oops . . . Oops . . . Oops . . . Oops . . .

"Why are my cookies spreading too thin or not spreading at all?" This is caused by the baking soda: Make sure you have used the required amount, no more and no less. If you have used the correct amount, then your soda may be too old, so try a fresh box. Remember, baking soda helps spread items and baking powder helps things rise. Getting them confused will cause an effect opposite from what you intended.

Coconut Macaroons

pictured on page 154

2 large egg whites
1/4 teaspoon cream of tartar
1/4 teaspoon vanilla extract

1 cup sugar
2 cups loosely packed sweetened
   flaked coconut

makes about 30 macaroons

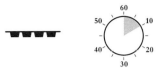

Preheat the oven to 300 degrees. Grease or spray with Pam 2 cookie sheets. Place the egg whites, cream of tartar and vanilla in a bowl. Beat with an electric beater at high speed until fluffy and stiff. Add the sugar a little at a time, beating constantly. Once the mixture is stirred and stiff, fold in the coconut with a spoon. Drop spoonfuls of the batter onto the greased cookie sheets. Bake at 300 degrees for about 20 minutes or until lightly golden. Remove from the cookie sheets very carefully (they are very delicate). Cool on a wire rack.

Oatmeal Cookies

pictured on page 154

3/4 cup butter-flavored
   shortening
1 cup packed brown sugar
1/2 cup sugar
1/4 cup water
1 tablespoon vanilla extract
2 eggs

1 1/2 cups flour
1/2 teaspoon salt
1/2 teaspoon baking soda
1 1/2 teaspoons cinnamon
3 cups uncooked oats (I like to
   use Quaker or Murphy's
   Irish Oats)

makes 3 dozen cookies

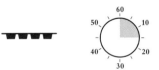

Beat together the shortening, sugars, water and vanilla until smooth and creamy. Add the remaining ingredients 1 at a time in the order given, mixing each into the batter before adding another. Drop tablespoonfuls of dough onto a greased cookie sheet. Bake in a preheated 350-degree oven for 13 minutes or until golden in color.

Variations

- Mix in 1 cup chocolate chips for **Chocolate Oatmeal Cookies.**
- Mix in 1 cup raisins for **Oatmeal Raisin Cookies.**
- Add 1 cup chopped walnuts to the basic recipe and each variation for 3 more ideas.

Peanut Butter Cookies

pictured on page 154

makes 3 dozen cookies

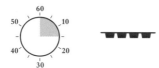

1 cup sugar
1 cup butter, softened
3 eggs
1 tablespoon vanilla extract
1 cup peanut butter

2¹/₂ cups flour
1 teaspoon baking powder
1 teaspoon baking soda
1 teaspoon salt

Beat the sugar and butter together until smooth. Add the eggs 1 at a time. Add the vanilla and peanut butter and mix well. Mix all the other dry ingredients in a bowl and add to the egg mixture; beat well. Refrigerate the dough for 30 minutes. Preheat the oven to 350 degrees. Shape the dough into golf ball-sized balls. Place 3 inches apart on an ungreased cookie sheet. Flatten the tops of the balls with a floured fork. Bake for 12 minutes or until lightly browned.

Variations

- For **Chocolate-Kissed Peanut Butter Cookies,** use the same recipe and roll the balls in sugar before placing on the cookie sheet; do not flatten. Bake for the same amount of time. When done, press a chocolate candy kiss firmly on the top of each cookie.
- For **Strawberry-Filled Peanut Butter Cookies,** use the same recipe and place the balls on the cookie sheet. Instead of flattening them, press an indentation into the middle of each cookie with your thumb. Fill the indentations with strawberry jam and bake as above.

Brownies

pictured on page 56

makes about 15 brownies

¹/₂ cup butter
4 ounces semisweet chocolate
1 cup sugar
2 large eggs

¹/₄ teaspoon salt
1 teaspoon vanilla extract
³/₄ cup flour
³/₄ cup chopped nuts (optional)

Melt the butter and chocolate in a saucepan over medium-low heat. Remove from the heat. Add the remaining ingredients in the order given, mixing each well before adding another. Pour into a buttered 8x8x2-inch baking dish. Bake in a preheated 350-degree oven for 30 minutes or until the edges seem dry and baked. The center will still be soft, but it will firm as it cools. Cool before cutting.

Apricot Squares

1¹/₄ cups flour
¹/₄ teaspoon salt
1 cup packed brown sugar
³/₄ cup butter

¹/₂ cup shredded coconut
³/₄ cup uncooked oats
¹/₂ cup chopped walnuts
1 (8-ounce) jar apricot preserves

serves 8

Mix the flour, salt, brown sugar and butter in a large bowl until it resembles a coarse meal. Stir in the coconut, oats and walnuts. Press 3 cups of the mixture into an ungreased 8-inch square pan. Cover completely with the apricot preserves. Press the remaining crust mixture evenly over the preserves. Bake in a preheated 325-degree oven for 1 hour. Cool and then cut into squares to serve.

Variation

- Try this with different types of preserves, such as raspberry, strawberry or blueberry.

Lemon Squares

1 cup uncooked quick oats
1 cup flour
¹/₂ cup flaked coconut
¹/₂ cup chopped pecans or
    walnuts
¹/₂ cup packed light brown sugar

1 teaspoon baking powder
¹/₂ cup butter
1 can condensed milk
¹/₂ cup ReaLemon reconstituted
    lemon juice
1 tablespoon grated lemon peel

serves 8

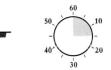

Mix the oats, flour, coconut, nuts, sugar, baking powder and butter in a mixing bowl. Spread half the mixture in a greased 9x9-inch baking pan. Mix the milk, lemon juice and lemon peel in another bowl. Pour over the layer in the pan. Cover with the remaining flour mixture. Bake in a preheated 350-degree oven for 30 minutes or until lightly browned. Let cool before cutting into squares.

Almond Dreams

pictured on page 154

makes about 3 dozen cookies

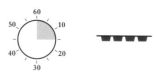

¹/₂ cup whole natural almonds	¹/₂ cup butter
1 cup flour	¹/₃ cup sugar
¹/₂ teaspoon baking powder	1 teaspoon almond extract
¹/₄ teaspoon salt	1 tablespoon water

Reserve 36 whole almonds. Chop the remaining almonds. Mix with the remaining ingredients in a large bowl. Roll the dough into 36 balls. Place 1 of the reserved almonds on the top of each ball. Place 2 inches apart on a greased cookie sheet. Bake in a preheated 350-degree oven for 20 minutes or until browned.

Dixie Bourbon Balls

makes 4 dozen balls

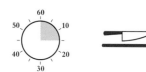

¹/₄ cup baking cocoa	1 cup finely chopped pecans
3¹/₂ cups crushed vanilla wafers	¹/₃ cup bourbon
1 cup confectioners' sugar	¹/₃ cup light corn syrup

Mix the cocoa, crushed wafers, confectioners' sugar and pecans in a large bowl. Add the bourbon and corn syrup and mix well. Shape into 1-inch balls. You may roll the balls in a variety of things such as confectioners' sugar, cocoa, jimmies, colored sugar, crispy rice cereal and many others. Store in an airtight container.

Apple Pie

1/3 cup cold water
2 tablespoons cornstarch
1 cup sugar
1 tablespoon cinnamon

1 teaspoon nutmeg
6 cups sliced peeled apples
   (preferably Granny Smith)
2 ready-made pie pastries

serves 8

Combine the water, cornstarch, sugar, cinnamon, nutmeg and 2 cups of the apples in a saucepan. Bring to a boil over medium heat; reduce the heat. Cook until the mixture begins to thicken; remove from the heat. Add the remaining apples. Place 1 pie pastry in a greased pie plate. Fill with the apple mixture. Cover with the remaining pie pastry, sealing the 2 crusts together by pinching the ends. Make 2 slits in the top crust for steam to escape during baking. Place in a preheated 400-degree oven. Bake for 45 to 60 minutes or until the crust is browned and filling is bubbling. Cool before serving.

Variations

- All fruit pies begin the same way as this one with the water, cornstarch, sugar and 6 cups of the chosen fruit. Omit the spices when making anything other than apple pies. For **Blueberry Pie,** heat until thickened: water, cornstarch, sugar and 2 cups of the blueberries. Once thickened, add the remaining blueberries. Bake as directed.
- **Strawberry Rhubarb Pie** uses 3 cups strawberries and 3 cups rhubarb. Use 1 cup of each for the boiling process and add the remainder after thickening. Bake as directed.
- The same would be true for **Peach, Cherry** or **Raspberry Pie.** Try one of your own or mix a few fruits for a combination of flavors, such as **Apple Raspberry.**

Chocolate Cream Pie

pictured on page 56

serves 8

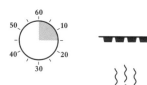

1 ready-made pie pastry
1/2 cup sugar
1/4 cup cornstarch
1/2 teaspoon salt
1/4 cup cold milk
3 large egg yolks

2 cups scalded milk
2 tablespoons butter
1 teaspoon vanilla extract
3 ounces semisweet chocolate
   morsels

Place the pie pastry in a buttered pie dish. Bake at 350 degrees for 10 minutes or until browned. Set aside to cool. Combine the remaining ingredients in a saucepan in the order given, mixing well after each is added. Cook over medium heat until thickened, stirring constantly; remove from the heat. Mix again with an electric mixer to avoid lumps. Pour into the pie pastry. Chill for 1 hour before serving. I like to top with whipped topping; use as much as you like. Garnish with chocolate jimmies.

Variation

- To make **Banana Cream Pie,** omit the chocolate and add 3 sliced ripe bananas after beating with the electric mixer.

Oops . . . Oops . . . Oops . . . Oops . . .

If your filling came out very lumpy or not thickened, you either didn't add the ingredients in order, or you didn't mix the ingredients well enough after each addition.

Oatmeal Pie

pictured on page 154

1 ready-made pie pastry
   (I prefer Pillsbury)
2 large eggs
1/2 cup sugar
1/2 cup packed brown sugar
1/4 cup corn syrup

3/4 cup uncooked oats
3/4 cup sweetened flaked
   coconut
1/2 cup milk
1 teaspoon vanilla extract
3 tablespoons butter

serves 6

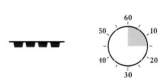

Preheat the oven to 350 degrees. Place the pie pastry in a greased pie dish and set aside. Beat the eggs in a bowl. Add the remaining ingredients in the order given, mixing well after each addition. Pour into the pie pastry. Bake for 40 minutes or until the filling is set except at the very center. It will continue to set while cooling.

Variations

- Add 1/4 cup oats and replace the coconut with 3/4 cup chocolate morsels for **Oatmeal Chocolate Pie.**
- Add in 1/2 cup chopped pecans for **Pecan Oatmeal Pie.**

Pecan Pie

pictured on page 154

3 large eggs
1 cup sugar
1/4 teaspoon salt
1/4 cup butter

1 cup dark corn syrup
1 1/2 cups chopped pecans
1 (9 inch) homemade or ready-
   made pie pastry

serves 8

Preheat the oven to 400 degrees. Beat the eggs with a hand mixer at high speed in a large mixing bowl. Add the sugar, salt, butter and corn syrup in the order given. Line a 9-inch pie pan with the pie pastry. Arrange the pecans in the pie pastry. Pour the sugar mixture over the pecans. Bake for 15 minutes. Reduce the oven temperature to 350 degrees. Bake for 25 minutes. The filling should be slightly soft in the very center; it will continue to firm up as it cools.

Sweet Potato Pie

pictured on page 154

serves 6

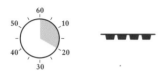

1 ready-made pie pastry
2 large eggs
1 1/2 cups mashed sweet potatoes
1 tablespoon butter
3/4 cup packed brown sugar

1 teaspoon cinnamon
1/2 teaspoon ground nutmeg
1 (12-ounce) can evaporated milk
1 teaspoon vanilla extract
2 tablespoons honey

Preheat the oven to 425 degrees. Place the pie pastry in a greased pie plate and set aside. Mix the remaining ingredients together in a large mixing bowl until as smooth as possible. Pour the filling into the pie pastry. Bake for 15 minutes. Reduce the oven temperature to 300 degrees. Bake for 25 minutes. The filling should be fairly soft in the very center; it will continue to set as it cools.

Variation

- To make **Pumpkin Pie** just replace the sweet potatoes with one 16-ounce can of solid-packed pumpkin and add another egg.

Pastry Pie Crusts

makes 2 crusts

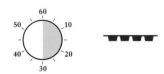

2 cups all-purpose flour
1 teaspoon salt

3/4 cup shortening
3 tablespoons cool water

Mix all the ingredients into a ball with a fork. Cool in the refrigerator for 10 minutes before rolling out. Separate into 2 balls. Roll out for a top and a bottom crust. To prebake a bottom crust, fit into a pie plate, line with waxed paper and fill with dried beans, rice or pie weights. Bake at 450 degrees for 8 to 10 minutes or just until firm. Remove the beans and waxed paper and bake for 5 minutes longer or until brown. If prebaking is not necessary, bake after filling.

Linzer Torte

1 cup butter, softened
1 cup sugar
2 egg yolks, beaten
1 1/2 cups chopped natural
  almonds

1 teaspoon grated lemon peel
2 cups flour
1 tablespoon cinnamon
1/2 teaspoon ground cloves
1 cup raspberry jam

serves 8

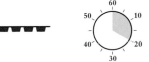

Beat the butter and sugar until smooth. Add the egg yolks, almonds and lemon peel. Blend in the remaining ingredients except the jam. Press half the mixture over the bottom and halfway up the side of a 9-inch springform pan. Spread with the jam. Roll the remaining dough into a rectangle. Cut into eight 1-inch wide strips and crisscross over the jam. Bake in a preheated 350-degree oven for 35 minutes. Cool and cut into wedges before serving.

Variations

- Use another flavor jam, such as strawberry, apricot or blackberry.
- Dip these strips halfway into melted chocolate for an added treat. You may even choose to roll the strips in nuts or coconut once dipped in the chocolate.

Crème Caramel

serves 8

1/2 cup sugar
4 large eggs
1 tablespoon vanilla extract

2 1/2 cups heavy cream
1/4 cup sugar

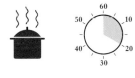

Pour 1/2 cup sugar into a 9-inch round baking pan. Heat over medium-high heat for 6 minutes or until the sugar is dissolved and brownish. Shake the pan a couple of times as it dissolves; do not stir. Remove from the heat. Mix the remaining ingredients in a bowl. Pour over the dissolved sugar and cover with foil. Preheat the oven to 350 degrees. Place the pan in the center of a shallow roasting pan filled with 1 inch of water. Bake for about 50 minutes or until a knife inserted in the center comes out clean. Remove the baking pan from the water; cool for 30 minutes. Loosen the custard from the side of the pan with a rubber spatula. Invert the custard onto a serving plate. The sugar should seep down the sides. Serve in slices with fresh whipped cream.

Indian Pudding

pictured on page 136

serves 8

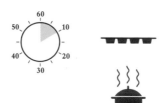

4 cups milk
2 tablespoons butter
1/2 cup yellow cornmeal
1/4 cup molasses
1/2 cup packed light brown sugar
1/2 teaspoon salt

1 teaspoon cinnamon
1/2 teaspoon ground ginger
1/4 teaspoon ground fresh
   nutmeg
1/2 teaspoon vanilla extract

Preheat the oven to 325 degrees. Butter a 2-quart casserole. Bring the milk and butter to a boil in a saucepan. Remove from the heat and stir in the cornmeal and molasses. Return to a boil over medium-high heat, stirring constantly. Remove from the heat. (The mixture should have thickened up at this point.) Stir in the brown sugar, salt, cinnamon, ginger, nutmeg and vanilla. Pour into the casserole. Bake for 30 minutes. Remove from the oven and give it a quick stir; return to the oven. Bake for 1 hour longer. Let stand to cool for 40 minutes before serving. Serve it warm with ice cream or cold with whipped cream.

Oops . . . Oops . . . Oops . . . Oops . . .

If your pudding is lumpy, next time whip in the cornmeal and molasses before returning it to the heat.

Vanilla Pudding

1 cup sugar
1/4 cup cornstarch
1/2 teaspoon salt
2 1/2 cups cold milk

3 egg yolks, beaten
1 tablespoon butter
2 tablespoons vanilla extract

serves 6

Combine the sugar, cornstarch and salt in a saucepan and stir in the milk and eggs. Bring the mixture to a boil over medium heat, stirring constantly. Remove from the heat and add the butter and vanilla. Let cool before serving.

Variations

- For **Chocolate Pudding,** add 2 ounces baking chocolate during the heating process.
- To make that ever popular **Tipsy Pudding,** layer some sliced pound cake, fresh or frozen strawberries and some of this pudding in a clear bowl. Add just a little brandy to float on top of the pudding. Repeat the layers once more and top the whole thing with whipped cream. The ratio of ingredients is up to you: If you like pudding, add more; add additional cake for a more "cakey" taste; if you don't want the brandy, don't add it.
- For **Rice Pudding,** add 1/2 cup uncooked converted rice and 1/2 cup heavy cream during the heating process and continue as directed.

Entertaining

Entertain: To keep the interest of and give pleasure to; to divert; to amuse; to give hospitality to; to have as a guest

Wine: The fermented juice of grapes, used as an alcoholic beverage and in cooking; juice having an intoxicating or exhilarating effect

Beer: An alcoholic fermented beverage made from grains, especially malted barley, and flavored with hops

The oldest and most widespread alcoholic drink in the world, beer was created by the Egyptians 3,000 years before Christ. In the thirteenth century Bavarian monks began adding hops to the fermentation process, which introduced flavors into their beer, now made popular once again with the craze of microbrews and home brewing.

Entertaining

Pictured on overleaf (recipe page numbers can be found in the index):

Perfect Baked Potatoes, Ginger Broccoli, Barbecue Calzone (a variation of Grilled Barbecue Pizza), Honey and Beer Baked Ham, Super Easy Cheesecake

All these dishes were prepared using the Baking, Boiling, Grilling, and Sautéing techniques.

Entertaining

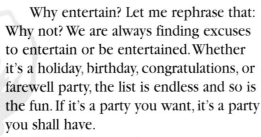

Why entertain? Let me rephrase that: Why not? We are always finding excuses to entertain or be entertained. Whether it's a holiday, birthday, congratulations, or farewell party, the list is endless and so is the fun. If it's a party you want, it's a party you shall have.

One of the most frequent questions I hear as a chef is, "How do you do it?" Most people have a hard time cooking for family, never mind for ten or more guests. If you're among the fortunate ones able to solve the problem with the magic word *caterer*, then you're lucky. Let's face it— caterers are expensive and hard to find. If you find one who is reputable and has good food, it's gonna cost you a fortune. Since for the most part selecting a caterer is a fifty-fifty chance of having a good experience, I'd rather just do it myself.

One of the biggest miscues in hosting a party is not allowing yourself enough time to do all that needs to be done. Entertaining is a lot of fun, but it does require some work and planning to make it successful. There are all sorts of styles of entertaining: casual, formal, informal. But all types of entertaining and all occasions (birthday, anniversary, etc.) have one thing in common: the attempt to extend a warm welcome to all the guests and to put them at ease in a setting of friendship and reverence toward the occasion honored. Where there's a crowd of people, there's food.

Entertaining is a lot like cooking— you don't start with a soufflé when you can't even make eggs. Start with a small party and work your way up. The first step to good entertaining is to pick what style of party it will be.

Casual parties are by far the most simple. These consist of get-togethers like barbecues, potluck dinners, and Super Bowl parties—or simply some friends getting together for dinner. (Seems very similar to things we do every day.) These parties are usually thrown together at the last minute, and you invite your guests by phone. I have these all the time, and I'm sure you've had them as well. I always seem to cook more food than I need to and at the last minute will invite a few friends over to help consume the meal. As much as it seems to be everyday living, it's still entertaining (in its simplest form). Food for these parties can be homemade or take-out or a mixture of the two. It might even be that each guest is bringing something. Plates and utensils can be anything from plastic and paper to your everyday ware. If it suits the mood, it's the right kind. Whenever I decide to use plastic and paper plates, I like to pick up quality products with festive patterns appropriate for the party.

Informal entertaining has a wide range of meanings. These parties require some planning and advance notice to the guests. Invitations should be sent out two weeks prior to the event. Informal parties include holiday get-togethers, birthdays, dinner parties, showers, etc. When preparing for an event like this, you should plan out a guest list; what type of meal (for example, dinner, brunch, appetizers only); the food to be served; and what, if any, decorations and table settings to use. Plan to include some dishes that can be made ahead of time so that you, too, can enjoy the party. It is also acceptable to buy some of the dishes being served. (I like to go to my favorite bakery and pick up dessert, but I have also been known to pick up appetizers at my favorite restaurant.) Appetizers are always a good way to start out the party. Whether you serve your main dishes in sitdown or buffet style, you should do it in courses. Before dessert comes out, clean up the main meal's mess; it makes for a much more relaxed dessert time, and a clean table is always more appealing than a dirty one.

Formal parties are the fancy ones you can never get your significant other to go to, because it means pulling out the top hat and gown. I have to admit that I like going to these parties a few times a year, but wouldn't want to do it on a regular basis. These parties are usually done for weddings, anniversaries, fund raisers, and New Year's Eve, to name just a few. They are rarely held at your home, but are usually done at banquet halls, clubs, or other rented spaces. For a formal party, it is imperative to mail invitations and request RSVPs. We RSVP most of the time because the food is catered, and each person means money. If you have ever planned a reception for a wedding, you know the time involved in putting together a party like this. Details include everything from the food to the music to the guests to the rented space to the caterer. In general, for this type of party, you're going to need help planning—anyone attempting this alone should be checked at the nearest mental health clinic! If you *are* planning it alone, prepare to spend lots of time on it.

I can't stress enough that planning is the key to any good party. Next most critical is the food. When planning food, no matter what the dish is, make sure that you have plenty to feed your guests. There's nothing worse than being caught short at a party, especially if it's yours. You can always plan around the basic premise that people in general are gluttons and take more than they can eat!

There are some basics to consider in menu planning as well. Try to think of each food's appearance—you want good shapes and colors. For instance, a broiled fish with a colorful tropical fruit chutney is more appealing than just the fish without the chutney. Texture of the food is also important. You wouldn't want to have a creamy chicken dish served with mashed potatoes and puréed squash, because it's all too runny to be placed together. Instead, you may want that creamy chicken with baby peas and roasted red bliss potatoes. You wouldn't serve a soft chip with salsa, but rather a crisp one. Complementing the flavors and richness of foods is tricky and takes a lot of practice, but it can be accomplished. Combine bland foods with flavorful ones; serve spicy foods with cooling agents (like sour cream as a cooler for chili). Try not to serve too many dishes with similar consistencies. You wouldn't serve a cream soup, then a creamed main dish with creamed carrots, and then cheesecake for dessert. That's too rich, and more cream than one person should have to endure. A good combination might start with a salad, then perhaps a fairly light entrée like grilled swordfish, finally finishing off the meal with a rich dessert like a triple layer fudge cake.

Dietary needs and/or preferences are becoming increasingly important today.

How to Arrange an Attractive Plate

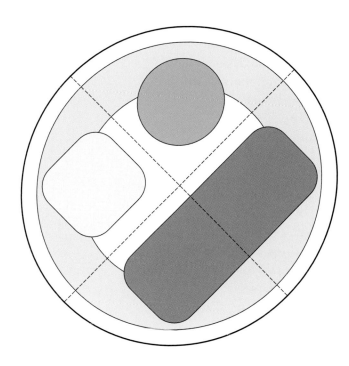

Vegetables offer great possibilities for contrasts in color, size, and shape.

- **●** whole (round: e.g., broiled tomatoes; long: asparagus or corn on the cob)

- **▲** mounds (e.g., potatoes, spinach—2 or 3 in contrasting colors are beautiful)

- **✿** irregularly shaped pieces (e.g., celery)

- **⁖** small, round pieces (e.g., green beans)

- **○** disks (e.g., sliced carrots)

- **❖** diced (e.g., eggplant)

- **||||** matchsticks (e.g., zucchini)

Mentally divide the plate into quarters. Fill two of them with a long main item (eg., a steak). Don't fill the other two with another long item, especially if the long item and the main food are similar colors (e.g., another brown food with the steak). Instead, use brightly colored vegetables in one quarter and mound a diced, crunchy food in the remaining quarter. If you fill up one quarter with the main item (e.g., a chicken breast), fill the other three with a brightly colored vegetable, a starch, and a salad. Remember, no matter what the main course might be or how many or few the accompaniments, the important thing is to be creative and present accompaniments whose color, texture, shape, and flavors provide a definite contast to the main item.

Or put a round, square, or triangular main item (e.g., a fish fillet) in the center. Surround with a sauce and several accompaniments.

Or ladle or drizzle sauce over the plate first and arrange the foods over the sauce.

The exception to the divided plate idea is dishes that are served alone (e.g., pasta or stir-fry). Place these foods at the center of the plate, leaving a clean 1/2 inch around the rim. Although a garnish is usually not needed, certainly a sprig of fresh basil or some other herb is acceptable. Any accompaniment to these dishes should be served separately as a side dish.

When you can see a lot of empty plate, the serving, no matter how generous, looks meager.

Study food photos in books and magazines, and watch television cooking shows. Copy the designs that appeal to you.

I always try to have at least one vegetarian dish, because, as a good host, I want to include my vegetarian friends in the fun.

This leads us to the most crucial factor in successful entertainment: you, the host. It's your duty to keep the party alive and fun, to make sure all the foods are presented, cooked, and cleared, and, most importantly, to make sure everyone knows one another. Because after all, what is entertaining but the invitation for guests to have a great time.

As a professional chef, I am frequently asked, "How do you know how much to make?" Well, I'm going to give you my formula for parties.

We are going to base this on a party for twenty people. The first thing I plan is a menu. How do I do that? Very simply, think of this book as a deal-a-meal with each of the techniques covered. This will prevent you from choosing only dishes that need to be prepared, say, in the oven. Pick items that can be done on the grill, in the oven, on the stove, or even simply cold. Basing around techniques will ensure that you will have enough cooking space and will provide your guests with a good variety of flavors. As a suggestion, go through the recipes in this book and, by using the icons, select and mix-and-match the recipes. This is by far the most important start of a party. If you don't have the space to cook, chaos will begin; and you certainly will not be hosting a party again for the sheer terror of it all.

Let's pretend we're going to serve three appetizers. I like to figure on three pieces per appetizer per person. Then the main dish. I always estimate that each person will consume about nine ounces of a main dish. For example, if you are having steak as the main dish, figure nine ounces per person. If we were to have three main dishes—steaks, swordfish, and pasta, perhaps—I would simply divide the nine ounces by the number of dishes to plan how much I would need. So, for this example, three dishes at three ounces per person per dish makes a total of sixty ounces per dish. Since sixteen ounces makes a pound, that gives us 3.7 pounds of pasta, steak, and swordfish that we have to get. If I get a number like 3.7, I will round up to four pounds because more is always safer than less.

Now that we know to plan on nine ounces per main dish, what about side dishes? Well, I simply do the same here but use the figure of six ounces per side dish per person. If I wanted two sides, I would need three ounces per person per dish. So if I had two side dishes for twenty people, that would be sixty ounces of each dish (which comes to 3.7 pounds per dish and again rounding up to four pounds per dish). When it comes to dessert, I always have a slice per person—there's no trick to this one.

No matter what it is that I am serving, I try to figure that each person will eat a little over a pound of food, but I break it down depending on the menu. If I were to have just an appetizer party, I would have a pound of appetizers per person. In review, each person requires approximately three ounces of an appetizer like a cup of soup or nine individual finger food appetizers, nine ounces of a main dish, six ounces of a side dish, and one dessert each. By using this and simply multiplying and dividing, you can easily figure out how much to buy.

Along with entertaining comes the practice of garnishing your food. No matter what the dish is, it can always be made to look more appetizing with a little added color. Some of the messiest dishes can be disguised with parsley and fruit slices to make them more attractive. It's always nice to be served a meal with a piece of flowering kale, or with a wedge of lemon or orange, something to add color to the plate. What it does for the plate, it will do for the whole dish as well.

Garnishes can be as simple as another food item, like topping a dish with a chutney or a salsa. A good example of this would be nachos—the melted cheese with olives, scallions, jalapeños, sour cream, and guacamole garnish the dish with an array of colors. Use garnishes that are edible to avoid sickness.

If you're going to garnish the table, I would recommend picking themes and garnish appropriately. For instance, if it's around Christmas time, I may place all around the empty table space cut-off trimmings of a Christmas tree, or holly and red and green candles. If it were around Halloween, pumpkins and cornstalks would be appropriate. In springtime I may put greens and assorted flower buds on the table to set a mood. (Take a look at the photos throughout this book to give you some creative ideas.)

And I can't say enough that there is no right or wrong way to do things; all that matters is if you like it or not. Once you get the hang of entertaining, you'll want to do it all the time—and you'll be praised by guests on how well you do it. So bon appétit!

More About Wines and Microbrews

The second biggest question after "How do I cook this dish?" is "What kind of wine can I serve with this dish?" Well, folks, at the risk of being redundant, I say that much like cooking, wine is an acquired taste as well as a matter of personal preference. Much like food, you know what you like and don't like—but you'll never know unless you try them. What I can offer is a little knowledge of what wines are, what makes one bottle better than another, and what the basic matches are for wine and food.

My first experience with wines began in high school with fruit-flavored wines and wine coolers. Then the step from Boone's Farm wine to white zinfandel came and I was off. Never having the appreciation for wines at an early age, my misconceptions were many. I hope to be able to clear up those misconceptions you too may have and help you enter the world of fine wines.

Let's start with how they actually make wine. Each winery may have many different growers, in different locations, and a wide variety of grapes. The wine process actually begins with these varieties because as the grapes arrive at the wineries, each specific grower and lot (the area where the grape is from) is kept and labeled separately. The grapes are then crushed, which means they are mechanically split open and placed in large stainless steel tanks with yeasts to start the fermentation process. Mind you, they are all labeled throughout each process and consistently kept separate.

Wining and Dining Wine Guide

The pairing of good food with fine wine is one of the great pleasures of life. The rule that you drink white wine only with fish and fowl and red wine with meat no longer applies—just let your own taste and personal preference be the guide. Remember to serve light wines with lighter foods and full-bodied wines with rich foods so the food and wine will complement rather than over-power each other.

Food and Wine Pairings

Semidry White Wines	Dove, quail, fish or shellfish in cream sauce Roast turkey, duck or goose Seafood, pasta or salad Fish in herbed butter sauce
Dry White Wines	Roast young game birds and waterfowl Shellfish Fried and grilled fish
Light Red Wines	Mild game sausage Fowl with highly seasoned stuffings Soups and stews Hare Creole foods
Hearty Red Wines	Duck and goose Game birds Venison, wild boar and hare Game soups and pies

Being able to keep them all separate allows the wineries to judge each lot's grapes. Some of these judgments include which ones are fantastic, which are consistently good, and which are not up to their desired quality.

If grapes don't meet the wineries' standards, projections can be made for the following year (for example, do they need a new supplier? do they need to change the crops? or should they adjust the soils?). Many questions are answered by keeping things separate and labeled.

The type of wine will determine how long it stays in those stainless tanks—anywhere from eight weeks to three months or longer.

Once the winemaker allots the time in tanks, they are transferred to American or French oak barrels where the fermentation process is completed (again, the type of wine being made will depend on the type of barrel it rests in). The barrel's core is toasted by fire to increase the oak flavors absorbed by the wine. Obviously, a mild, light wine should not spend its remaining time in a dark roasted barrel, because the flavor of the barrel would overcome the flavor of the wine and create a new tone that may not be desired.

In general, most wines will complete their barrel aging in eighteen months; again, the make of wine will coincide with the length of time it ferments. During this last step before bottling, many tests are done to create the wine you have on the table. This is where all that labeling becomes so important. The winemakers take samples of each of the lots and begin their blending process. The winemakers, however, will be merciless to the crop of grapes because the quality of the grape will determine the quality of the wine. Weather and proper vine attendance have the most influence on the quality of the grape. It is here that the winemaker will judge the quality of the grapes from that harvest. If it is an exceptional year, let's say for the Merlot grape, the winemaker may decide to make a reserve for that year. Thus, when you see "reserve" on a bottle of wine, you will know that was an exceptional year for that particular grape in that particular winery. It does not mean, however, that they will have a reserve wine of the same sort for the following year.

After the winemakers have judged the quality of the grape, they next decide which lots are going to be used for what wine. To help you understand this a little better, each wine is a blend of lots and grapes. For example, a bottle labeled Merlot must be within the guidelines made for all wineries; the blend must have a certain percentage of Merlot grapes in it to be called Merlot. And to be labeled a Sonoma or Napa wine, all the grapes must come from that area. One of my biggest surprises came when I found out that red or white "table wine" didn't mean that it was a cheap wine. It just means that the blend of grapes did not fall into any category of labeled wine. It is very well possible to have a great blend of grapes produce a fantastic so-called table wine. So don't be stuck in the same frame of mind that I was. I've come to appreciate red and white table wines and like them as much if not more in some circumstances than a bottle of Merlot or Chardonnay.

Only so much of each wine is made depending on the harvest. Let's take Merlot for an example, but the same is true for any other wine as well. The wine-maker either has an idea for taste, or a sample Merlot of the prior year. Based on this knowledge, he goes to where the barrels are kept and tastes each of the lots' samples to decide which lots he wants to use for his blend to make that famous Merlot everyone has grown to love. This is where things can get a bit tricky, because the winemaker is reliant on the crop of the season. Any year's product will not be the same as the year past and will not be the same as the year to come—no matter how much they try to duplicate, or improve, the Merlot each year.

The winemaker decides which lots to use for the Merlot of the year. This is where the availability of the wine comes into effect. Let's say he uses the lot marked number one as his base grape and two and three to blend in to make that bottle

Semidry White Wines

These wines have a fresh fruity taste and are best served young and slightly chilled.

Johannisberg Riesling—	(*Yo-hann-is-burg Rees-ling*)
Frascati—	(*Fras-cah-tee*)
Gewürztraminer—	(*Ge-vert-tram-me-ner*)
BernKasteler—	(*Barn-kahst-ler*)
Sylvaner Riesling—	(*Sil-vah-nur Rees-ling*)
Est! Est! Est!	
Fendant—	(*Fahn-dawn*)
Dienheimer—	(*Deen-heim-er*)
Krauznacher—	(*Kroytz-nock*)

Dry White Wines

These wines have a crisp, refreshing taste and are best served young and slightly chilled.

Vouvray—	(*Voo-vray*)
Chablis—	(*Shab-lee*)
Chardonnay—	(*Shar-doh-nay*)
Pinot Blanc—	(*Pee-no Blawn*)
Chenin Blanc—	(*Shay-nan Blawn*)
Pouilly Fuisse—	(*Pwee-yee Fwee-say*)
Orvieto Secco—	(*Orv-yay-toe Sek-o*)
Piesporter Trocken—	(*Peez-porter*)
Meursault—	(*Mere-so*)
Hermitage Blanc—	(*Air-me-tahz Blawn*)
Pinot Grigio—	(*Pee-no Gree-jo*)
Verdicchio—	(*Ver-deek-ee-o*)
Sancerre—	(*Sahn-sehr*)
Soave—	(*So-ah-veh*)

Light Red Wines

These wines have a light taste and are best served young at cool room temperature.

Beaujolais—	*(Bo-sho-lay)*
Bardolino—	*(Bar-do-leen-o)*
Valpolicella—	*(Val-po-lee-chel-la)*
Moulin-A-Vent Beaujolais—	*(Moo-lon-ah-vahn)*
Barbera—	*(Bar-bear-ah)*
Lambrusco—	*(Lom-bruce-co)*
Lirac—	*(Lee-rack)*
Nuits-Saint Georges "Villages"—	*(Nwee San Zhorzh)*
Gamay Beaujolais—	*(Ga-mai Bo-sho-lay)*
Santa Maddalena—	*(Santa Mad-lay-nah)*
Merlo di Ticino—	*(Mair-lo dee Tee-chee-no)*

Hearty Red Wines

These wines have a heavier taste, improve with age, and are best opened thirty minutes before serving.

Barbaresco—	*(Bar-bah-rez-coe)*
Barolo—	*(Bah-ro-lo)*
Zinfandel—	*(Zin-fan-dell)*
Chianti Riserva—	*(Key-ahn-tee Ree-sairv-ah)*
Cote Rotie—	*(Coat Ro-tee)*
Hermitage—	*(Air-me-tahz)*
Taurasi—	*(Tah-rah-see)*
Merlot—	*(Mair-lo)*
Syrah—	*(Sir-rah)*
Chateauneuf-Du-Pape—	*(Shot-toe-nuff dew Pop)*
Petite Sirah—	*(Puh-teet Seer-rah)*
Cote de Beaune—	*(Coat duh Bone)*
Cabernet Sauvignon—	*(Cab-air-nay So-vin-yawn)*

of Merlot. Even though he may have lot numbers four and five of the same variable, he doesn't use them to create more Merlot. Thus, when lot one has run out of the base ingredient, then that is the number of Merlot bottles they will have for sale for that season. Don't worry—the other wine is not thrown out but rather is either blended to make another wine or is sold to another winery to make a blend of their own.

Once they have decided on the blend that they are going to use, it goes to bottling and labeling, and then eventually to you. On average each harvest arrives to us two years after being harvested. So remember, if you like a bottle of Merlot from 1997 from let's say Benzinger, Sonoma, you better get it now; when the 1998 comes out, it won't be that '97 that you love—it may be close but it will be a different grape and thus a different flavor. I usually like to buy the reserves when they come out, because they're limited, and I know that it's a special blend that is not usually made each year, but only in exceptional years.

I always wondered, "How long will a bottle of wine keep?" or "How long can I wait to drink this bottle?" Unfortunately, there is no easy answer to this question, but here are some suggestions. First of all, proper storage will help preserve the wine, but won't guarantee the shelf life. Secondly, the wine must be kept stored on its side to allow the moisture to be received by the cork. Cork is a porous, live material that comes from a cork tree. So if the liquid is not in contact with the cork, the cork will dry out and then the seal with the wine may be broken. In other words, if the cork dries out, oxygen will be allowed to enter the bottle and thus the oxidation of the wine will eventually ruin that bottle. The bottles should also be kept in a dark, cool place. Light can cause a chemical reaction that would alter the flavor of the wine.

Wine is a very temperamental blend that will also be altered by a drastic change in temperature. The best comparison is beer. If you take a beer from a cooler, go to the beach, and don't drink it, then it will become the temperature of the beach weather. Well, you get home and put the beer back in the refrigerator; two days later when you go to drink it, you will find it's been "skunked." Wine is not much different from beer—you either keep it cold or in a controlled temperature environment. This is where wine cellars came into play—dark, cool, and never rising above 55 degrees are the best conditions for storing wine. However, the key is keeping that temperature consistent (preferably under 60 degrees). So with all these factors playing into the shelf life of the bottle you want to store, each person's treatment and storage of wine will play a role in its life. For the most part, wine should be drunk right away, although some may be able to last many years depending on the wine, the cork, the light exposure, and the temperature control. If your wine does turn to vinegar, don't throw it out: Bring it to a boil on the stove, let it cool down, and you've got yourself your own homemade wine vinegar. Good luck on saving your wines—it's always hard to save that bottle when you know how good it is. So the question may not be how long can I save it, but how long can I survive the torture of not drinking that fabulous bottle of wine.

Cooking with Wine

Cooking with wine is a time-honored culinary tradition, but many novice cooks (and some not so novice cooks) are at a loss to know how to begin. Help is on the way!

Guidelines on when and how much to add

- For soups, stir in 1 tablespoon of wine per serving just before serving time. Meat-based and vegetable-based soups are enhanced by dry sherry, medium sherry, or dry red wine. Add sherry or dry white wine to cream-based soups.

- Use dry white wine or vermouth with fish. Baste broiled or baked fish with a mixture of equal amounts of wine or vermouth and melted butter. Poach fish in equal parts wine or vermouth and water.

- Equal parts dry white wine, dry red wine, vermouth, or sherry should be used to frequently baste broiled chicken. Add dry white wine, dry red wine, or vermouth to a stew at the same time you add the browned chicken.

- Game birds may be basted occasionally with 1/4 cup dry red wine per pound.

- Baste a baked ham with 1 to 2 cups of a sweet dessert wine (such as port or muscatel) at the point where the recipe calls for glazing. Add 1/4 cup of light or dark madeira to braised ham immediately after browning.

- Braised, stewed, or roasted beef or lamb will be savory if you add 1/4 cup dry red wine per pound after the meat has been browned. Use dry white wine for veal or lamb.

- When preparing sauces, add the wine when you add the other liquid ingredients. Perk up cream-based sauces with 1 tablespoon dry sherry, medium sherry, or dry white wine per each cup of sauce. Tomato-based sauces need sherry or dry red wine.

- When preparing gravy for meat or poultry, add about 2 tablespoons dry red wine, dry white wine, or sherry per cup when you add other liquids. Be sure to boil well.

- Heighten the flavor of fresh, frozen, or canned fruit by adding 1 tablespoon of a sweet wine (such as muscatel or sauterne) per cup of fruit. Let stand for 30 minutes or so or until the wine has permeated the fruit. Or pour a sparkling wine or still wine over fresh fruit immediately before serving.

Different types of wines and their pairing with foods are shown on page 186.

We have entered an age where abundant microbrews are the latest fad. Beers begin with malts and hops. Malts are sugars taken from the malted barley grains, and like the beer they produce, there are many varieties, from light to dark. Malts give the beer color and sweetness. Hops are almost the opposite of malts. They give beer its bitterness and also help clear the color of the beer.

The mix and match of the balance of these two main ingredients creates a wide variety of flavors and colors. That's not to mention other ingredients that are added to make new flavors, such as yeasts, water, sugar, and flavorings (raspberry, for example). So to make it easier for you to understand the differences, I have divided them up to make a little more sense.

Continental beers are lighter beers with a full body, a gold color, and a good malty taste that isn't very bitter. Heineken is a good example of this. Continental dark beers are a clear, darker brown color and are full bodied, but tend to be a bit drier rather than sweet. Heineken dark would be an example of this kind.

Pilsners are known for their lightness in both color and flavor with no bitterness. Pale ale is one of the most popular today. Ales range in color from golden to copper to amber but all have the distinctive combination of full-bodied malt taste and bitter hops. India pale ales are the most bitter of the bunch, while a light pale ale is generally lighter and also contains less alcohol than the regular ales.

Brown ales, like Newcastle, all tend to be the sweeter of the beers and often impart a fruitiness to them. Bock beers contain at least six percent alcohol, are dark brown in color, and have a sweet,

Wine, Beer, and Cheese Complements

Wine	or Beer	Cheese
Appetizer		
Blush	Indian Ale	Cheddar
Champagne		Fontina
Sherry		Gorgonzola
Vermouth		Gruyère
		Port Salut
Red		
Beaujolais	Boch	Bel Paese
Bordeaux	Porter	Cheddar
Burgundy	Stout	Edam
Cabernet Sauvignon	Brown Ale	Monterey Jack
Chianti		Piquant Bleu
Claret		Roquefort
Rosé		Swiss
Zinfandel		Tilsit
White		
Chablis	Pilsner	Boursin
Chardonnay	Golden Ale	Brie
Chenin Blanc	Copper Ale	Camembert
Moselle	Amber Ale	Creamy Bleu
Pouilly Fuisse		Gouda
Riesling		Gruyère
Sauterne		Montrachet
Sauvignon Blanc		Port Salut
Soave		Roquefort
Sparkling		
Champagne	Continental	Any of the cheeses listed to go with appetizer, red or white wines would be appropriate complements to any of the sparkling wines.
Cold Duck		
Sparkling Burgundy		
Sparkling Rosé		

Wine	Cheese
Dessert	
Cream Sherry	Brie
Muscatel	Camembert
Port	Cheddar
Sweet Sherry	Cream
Tokay	Liederkranz
	Roquefort
	Stilton

full-bodied flavor. Amber beers, like Sam Adams, are just a fuller-bodied pale ale that contains a lot of malt flavors.

Porters are dark brown beers that don't have the burned flavor of a stout; they tend to be a bit lighter and milder in flavor. Stouts are very dark with characteristics of taste to match. Smoky and full bodied with a full hop flavor, not all stouts are bitter; there are also sweet stouts.

Wheat beers are made with forty to seventy-five percent wheat, and are all light in color due to the wheat. They are cloudy in a golden tone and for the most part have a clove-like taste.

Regardless of the style of beer, flavors can be added to the beer to create a whole new taste. This is why we have raspberry wheats, nut ales, and so on. So, a lager is not a style of beer; it is a method of production. This is how we can get a light to dark beer and a light- to full-bodied beer.

With microbrews being the latest sensation, it seems only right to at least know the basics. If you don't like bitter beer, you wouldn't buy a stout; if you want a light beer, think pale ale. Much like wine, beer, too, is personal preference and takes trial and error to determine what we like and don't like.

Other Helpful Charts

Thawing Meat and Poultry

Meat	Thawing In Refrigerator
Large roasts and smoked meats over 4 pounds	4 to 7 hours per pound
Steaks, chops, ham slices	
1 inch	8 to 10 hours total
1^1/$_2$ inch	9 to 12 hours total
2 inch	11 to 14 hours total
Flank steak, whole	8 to 10 hours total
Spareribs, whole side	7 to 10 hours total

Poultry	Thawing In Refrigerator
Cut-up pieces	3 to 9 hours
Whole:	
Under 4 pounds	12 to 16 hours
4 to 12 pounds	24 to 48 hours
12 to 16 pounds	2 to 3 days
16 to 20 pounds	3 to 4 days
20 to 24 pounds	4 to 5 days

Temperatures You Should Know

How cold should I keep my freezer? The refrigerator? What in the world is room temperature? Here's help!

	Fahrenheit	Celsius
Warming oven	225 to 250	105 to 120
Very slow oven	275 to 300	135 to 150
Slow oven	325	165
Moderate oven	350 to 375	175 to 190
Moderately hot oven	400 to 425	205 to 220
Hot oven	450	235
Very hot oven	475	245
Extremely hot oven	500	260
Broiling	550	290
Freezer	0	-18
Refrigerator freezer	10	-12
Refrigerator	34 to 40	1 to 4
Wine storage	55	13
Room temperature	68	20
Temperature to cause dough to rise	80	25
Water simmers	180	80
Water boils	212	100

Fruits and Vegetables

Use this guide when planning fresh fruits and vegetables for your daily meals. Take advantage of best buys during peak seasons to stretch your food budget. Buy extras when they're most plentiful, and can or freeze them for off-season enjoyment.

Fruits	Plentiful or Near Peak	Vegetables	Plentiful or Near Peak
Apples	October through December	Beets	June through September
Apricots	June and July	Broccoli	November through March
Cantaloupe	June through September	Cauliflower	October and November
Cherries	June and July	Celery	October through June
Cranberries	October through December	Corn	June through September
Grapefruit	January through April	Cucumbers	May through August
Grapes	August through November	Green beans	May through August
Lemons	June and July	Mushrooms	November through January
Oranges	December through May	Peppers, green	June through August
Peaches	June through September	Potatoes, sweet	October through December
Pears	August through November	Radishes	March through May
Rhubarb	February through June	Rutabagas, Turnips	November through January
Strawberries	April through June		
Tangerines	November through January	Spinach	March and April
Watermelons	May through August	Squash, summer	June through August
		Squash, winter	September through November
		Tomatoes	May through August

Bananas, cabbage, carrots, onions, lettuce and potatoes usually are in good supply year-round.

Herbs and Spices

Herb or Spice	When to Use
Allspice	Pungent aromatic spice; whole or in powdered form. It is excellent in marinades, particularly in game marinade, or in curries. Also especially good in spice cake, yams, squash, pumpkin, pickles and stews.
Anise seeds	Seeds of annual plant from Spain, India, and Mexico. Source of licorice flavor used for baking, salads, seafood, and candy.
Basil	Can be chopped and added to cold poultry salads. If the recipe calls for tomatoes or tomato sauce, add a touch of basil to bring out a rich flavor.
Bay leaf	The basis of many French seasonings. It is added to soups, stews, marinades and stuffings. Must be removed after cooking.
Bouquet garni	A must in many Creole cuisine recipes. It is a bundle of herbs, spices and bay leaf tied together and added to soups, stews or sauces.
Caraway seeds	Brown seeds of biennial plant Carum carvi from Holland and North Africa. Crushed to make oil or liqueur. Used in rye bread, cakes, pastry, cheese, stewed meats, sauerkraut, salads, with potatoes and in main dishes.
Cardamom seeds	Aromatic seeds of the fruiting pod of a tropical herb. Adds sweetness to breads, pastries and cookies. An ingredient of condiment recipes.
Cayenne	Ground from small dried capsicums or chile peppers. Sometimes called red pepper. Very hot. Used in Mexican and Creole dishes and in casseroles, rice, sauces and with seafood.
Celery seeds	From wild celery rather than domestic celery. It adds pleasant flavor to bouillon or a stock base, coleslaw, potato salad, salad dressings, soups and stews.
Chervil	One of the traditional fines herbes used in French-derived cooking, chervil has a slight licorice flavor. (The other fines herbes are tarragon, parsley and chives.) It is good in omelets or soups.
Chili powder	Spanish recipe necessity made of chili pepper, oregano, cumin, garlic, and salt. Especially used for chili, mole sauce, and curry dishes.
Chives	The most delicate flavor in the onion family. Available fresh, dried or frozen, it can be substituted for raw onion or shallot in any poultry recipe.

Herbs and Spices

Herb or Spice	When to Use
Cinnamon	Ground from the bark of the cinnamon tree, it is important in desserts as well as savory dishes. Cinnamon sticks can be used in pickling, toddies and fancy coffees.
Cloves	Unopened, dried bud of an evergreen tree. Available whole and ground. Whole cloves used to stud ham, beef and onions. Ground cloves used in baking, casseroles, vegetables, desserts and sauces.
Coriander	A native Mediterranean seed. Adds an unusual flavor to soups, stews, chili dishes, curries, beef broth, meat sauces, gingerbread and spice cookies.
Cumin	This staple spice in Mexican cooking has an aromatic, slightly bitter taste. To use, rub seeds together and let them fall into the dish just before serving. Cumin also comes in powdered form. Used in meat dishes and pickling mixtures.
Curry powder	A blend of spices imported from Madras, India, which can include allspice, cardamom, fennel, mace, chili powder, cinnamon, cloves, coriander, cumin, fenugreek, ginger, nutmeg, cayenne pepper and turmeric. This seasoning ranges from mild to hot. Used with lamb, fish, poultry, rice, soups, venison, kidney stews, mushrooms, other vegetables and in sauces.
Dill	Another relative of parsley with delicate but spicy flavor. Use as seeds or dry leaves. Turns bitter when subjected to high heat. Used with dairy sour cream, fish and vegetables. Also used in pickling.
Fennel seeds	Classic herb used in Scandinavian hot breads, cakes and cookies. Also Italian sausage and Spanish dishes. Tastes like anise.
Garlic	One of the oldest herbs in the world, it must be carefully handled. For best results, press or crush garlic clove.
Ginger	Root of a perennial plant. Often used in Oriental cooking. Fresh root available whole or candied. Dried ginger available whole or ground. Whole ginger used in syrup, pickling, marinades and drinks. Ground ginger used in baking, main dishes, vegetables and desserts. Candied or crystallized ginger used in baking and desserts.
Juniper berries	Aromatic berries from an evergreen tree. Bitter, slightly resinous flavor. Used in stuffing and with game and gin.
Lemon peel (fresh or dried)	This is used in sauces, marinades for lamb, chicken and veal. Added to cake batters, dessert sauces, meringues and custards.

Herbs and Spices

Herb or Spice	When to Use
Lovage	Bittersweet, celery-like flavor. Use sparingly with meat and in soups, stews, casseroles and salads.
Mace	Aromatic ground fibrous covering of the nutmeg. Delightful addition to fruitcake, lemon desserts, cauliflower, spiced wine and eggnog.
Marjoram	A sweet spicy aromatic herb of the mint family, it is good in soups, sauces, stuffings and stews.
Mustard (dry)	Brings a sharp bite to sauces. Sprinkle just a touch over roast chicken for a delightful flavor treat.
Nutmeg	Aromatic dried seed of an evergreen tree from which the spice mace also comes. Available whole or ground. Used in main dishes, vegetables, soup, sauces and desserts.
Orange peel	Delectable in baking uses, duck and barbecue sauces. Also added to butter, syrups and honey for toppings.
Oregano	A staple herb in Italian, Spanish and Mexican cuisines. It is very good in dishes with a tomato foundation; it adds an excellent savory taste.
Paprika	A mild pepper that adds color to gravy, salad dressings and chili. Used as a garnish for salads, meats and casseroles. The very best paprika is imported from Hungary.
Parsley	The all-time favorite herb for seasoning and garnishing. Member of celery family. Flavorful stems used in stocks and bouquet garni. Leaves used to flavor any savory dish.
Pepper	Berries of a climbing tropical vine. Black, white, red and green available whole, ground or pickled (green). Used in savory dishes.
Poppy seeds	The Asian herb that has nutty tasting seeds and odor. Poppy seed cakes and cookies with filling are grand. Great on bread and rolls.
Rosemary	A tasty herb with a strong resinous flavor; important in seasoning stuffing for duck, partridge, capon and other poultry. Use in marinades in combination with wines.
Saffron	Dried stigma of saffron crocus. Slightly bitter. Available as threads or ground. Crush or dissolve in hot water. Used in risotto, paella, bouillabaisse, sauces, bread and some desserts.

Herbs and Spices

Herb or Spice	When to Use
Sage	Sharp, slightly bitter taste. A perennial favorite with all kinds of poultry and stuffings. It is particularly good with goose.
Sesame seeds	Small Oriental seeds with a nut-like flavor used as a bread and cake topping, in candies, and as a garnish on meat recipes.
Tarragon	One of the fines herbes. Goes well with all poultry dishes whether hot or cold. Has a licorice flavor.
Thyme	Delicately flavored. Usually used in combination with bay leaf in soups, stews and sauces.
Turmeric	It is the ground rhizome of an East Indian plant. Used to give brilliant yellow color to rice, soups, pickles, poultry, seafood and sauces.
Vanilla bean	A dried fruit of the vanilla orchid used whole as a flavoring stick in making desserts, candy and syrups. Also sold in liquid extract form.
Winter savory	Spicy, peppery flavor, less delicate than Summer Savory. Used with dried and fresh beans, rice, meat, fish and in stuffing and salad.

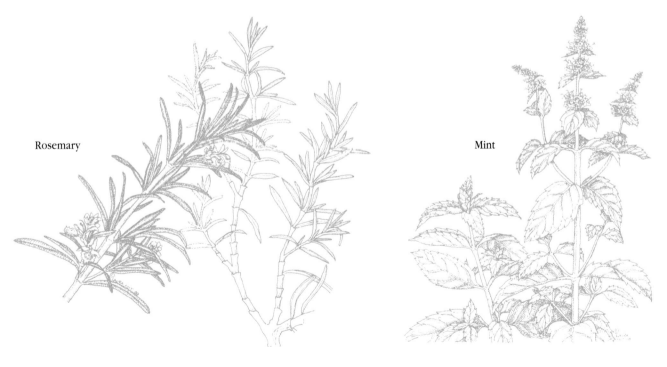

Rosemary

Mint

Herb and Spice Hints

Chives

Dill

Lavender

Use fresh herbs whenever possible; their flavor and aroma are superior to that of dried herbs.

To store fresh herbs, wrap them in a damp cloth or paper towel or place stems in fresh water and store in refrigerator.

Fresh herbs can be dried or frozen. Some can be preserved in vinegar. (A few herbs are sold frozen.)

To substitute dried herbs for fresh, reduce amount to one-third.

Store dried herbs in airtight containers, away from heat. Buy small quantities at a time and use within about six months.

Reconstitute dried herbs by briefly soaking them in a small amount of liquid or by heating in butter over low heat.

When a recipe is increased, do not automatically increase herbs in the same proportion as other ingredients. Season to taste.

Herbs should enhance the flavor of food, not overpower it.

Although fresh parsley is a beautiful garnish, other fresh herbs can also be used. Use the same herb to garnish that you have used for seasoning a dish.

Store spices in tightly covered containers in a cool, dark place.

Buy small quantities of spices and use within about six months.

When possible, buy whole spices; then grind just before using. Freshly ground spices have the best flavor.

Use spices sparingly. Spices should enhance, not overpower, the natural flavor of food. You can always add additional seasoning.

When adding whole spices to a recipe, tie them in a cheesecloth bag for easy removal before serving.

Be careful not to burn, scorch or overcook spices. Some of them become bitter when subjected to high heat or overcooking.

When a recipe is increased, do not automatically increase spices in the same proportion as other ingredients. Instead, season to taste to avoid overseasoning.

Shellfish Information Chart

Shellfish	Availability	Type	Cooking Methods
Clams	summer	mollusk	baking, steaming
Crabs	summer to winter	crustacean	braising, poaching, steaming
Lobster	spring to summer	crustacean	grilling, poaching, steaming
Mussels	early fall to spring	mollusk	baking, grilling, steaming
Oysters	early fall to spring	mollusk	baking, braising, broiling, frying, grilling
Scallops, Bay	fall	mollusk	baking, braising, broiling, frying, poaching, sautéing
Scallops, Sea	mid fall to spring	mollusk	baking, braising, broiling, frying, grilling, poaching, sautéing
Shrimp	year-round	crustacean	baking, braising, broiling, frying, grilling, poaching, sautéing, steaming

Buying Tips

All fresh shellfish should have a mild aroma and smell of the sea. Avoid shellfish that have a strong fishy odor. Fresh shellfish are very perishable. To find the freshest shellfish available, buy from a reputable fish market or supermarket that has a rapid turnover. If you are in doubt about the freshness of any shellfish, do not buy it. If you are purchasing live shellfish, it is best to buy them as close to the time you plan to cook them as possible. Fresh shellfish should be cooked on the day they are purchased.

Live lobsters and crabs should feel heavy for their size and actively move their claws. Lobsters should flap their tail tightly against their chests or hold their tail under their shell when picked up. However, if the lobsters and crabs have been refrigerated they will not be as active. Do not purchase any lobsters or crabs that do not show these signs of life. Shrimp are available raw or cooked, fresh or frozen, and unshelled or peeled. All should feel firm to the touch. Cooked shelled shrimp should be plump. Raw shrimp should not smell of ammonia. Clams, mussels and oysters should have moist shells free of cracks and chips. All hard-shell clams, mussels and oysters should have tightly closed shells or slightly open shells that snap tightly closed when tapped.

How Much to Buy Per Person

Lobster (in shell)—10 to 14 ounces
Large shrimp (unshelled)—10 ounces
Large shrimp (shelled)—3 ounces
Crab (in shell)—14 ounces to 1 pound

Oysters—6 to 12 individual
Scallops—8 to 10 ounces, or 6 to 12 in shells
Mussels, Clams—14 ounces, or 6 to 12 individual

Storage

Shellfish are highly perishable and it is best to use them within 24 hours of purchase. They need to be handled carefully before cooking to keep them fresh or alive. The most important factor is to keep them in a cold, moist environment. Keep fresh or thawed shellfish as close to 32 degrees Fahrenheit as possible.

Cheese Chart

Cheese is one of the oldest foods known to man and has appeared in some form wherever he has grazed animals and used their milk. The Persian philosopher, Zoroaster, is reputed to have lived for 20 years on cheese alone in the 6th century. Cheese is frequently mentioned in the Bible. The famous Gorgonzola cheese has been made in the Po Valley in Italy since 879 A.D., and the great monasteries of Europe were well known for cheese-making throughout the Middle Ages. Since that time, each country and region of the world has developed cheeses which are an integral part of their cooking and are readily identified with the cuisine of the country.

Cheese is a universal and almost-perfect food. It contains many of the essential food elements which the body needs, such as proteins, fats and vitamins. The rich variety of tastes makes it appealing to everyone—with the choice depending primarily on how it is to be used.

The important thing to remember when cooking with cheese is that excessive heat and prolonged cooking cause it to become stringy and leathery. High heat may also cause a mixture of cheese, eggs and milk to curdle. When making a sauce, add the cheese toward the end of the cooking time, stirring over low heat just long enough to melt and blend it with the other ingredients. A cheese topping should be broiled several inches away from the heat source. Casseroles with cheese should be baked at low to medium temperatures.

One pound of shredded cheese will measure four cups for use in recipes. One pound of soft cheese such as cottage cheese or cream cheese will measure two cups.

Cheese	Goes With	Used For	Flavor, Texture
American (U.S.)	Crackers	Cooking Sandwiches	Mild, Cheddar-type processed cheese
Bel Paese (Italy)	Fresh fruit French bread	Dessert Snack	Spongy, mild, creamy yellow interior
Bleu (France)	Fresh fruit Bland crackers	Dessert Dips, Salads	Marbled, blue-veined, semisoft, piquant
Boursin (France)	Dry white wines Fruity red wines	Snack	Soft, spreadable, triple-cream
Brick (U.S.)	Crackers Bread	Sandwiches Snack	Semisoft, mild, cream-colored to orange
Brie (France)	Fresh fruit	Dessert Snack	Soft, edible crust, creamy
Camembert (France)	Apples	Dessert Snack	Mild to pungent, edible crust, yellow

Cheese Chart

Cheese	Goes With	Used For	Flavor, Texture
Cheddar (England)	Fresh fruit Crackers	Dessert Cooking, Snack	Mild to sharp, cream-colored to orange
Chèvre (France)	White wine French bread	Cooking, Snack Salads	Moist and creamy to dry and semifirm
Chihuahua (Mexico)	Crackers Bread	Cooking	Soft, mild, similar to Monterey Jack
Colby (U.S.)	Fresh fruit Crackers	Cooking, Sandwiches Snack	Mild, sweet, lighter and softer than Cheddar
Cottage (U.S.)	Canned or Fresh fruit	Fruit salads Cooking	Soft, moist, mild, white
Cream (U.S.)	Crackers and Jelly	Dessert, Cooking Sandwiches	Soft, smooth, mild, white
Edam (Holland)	Fresh fruit	Dessert Snack	Firm, mild, red wax coating
Emmentaler (Switzerland)	Fresh fruit	Cooking, Dessert Snack	Mild, sweet, nutty, holes
Feta (Greece)	Greek salad	Salads Cooking	Salty, crumbly, white
Gorgonzola (Italy)	Fresh fruit Italian bread	Dessert Snack	Semisoft, blue-veined, piquant
Gouda (Holland)	Fresh fruit Crackers	Dessert Snack	Softer than Edam, mild, nutty
Gruyère (Switzerland)	Fresh fruit	Dessert Fondue	Nutty, bland, firm, tiny holes
Havarti (Denmark)	Crackers	Cooking, Sandwiches Snack	Rich, creamy, small holes, mild and tangy when young, sharper when aged
Liederkranz (Germany)	Onion slices Dark bread	Dessert Snack	Edible light orange crust, robust, soft

Cheese Chart

Cheese	Goes With	Used For	Flavor, Texture
Limburger (Belgium)	Dark bread Bland crackers	Dessert	Soft, smooth, white, robust, aromatic
Mascarpone (Italy)	Fresh fruit	Snack, Tiramisus	Very rich, creamy
Monterey Jack (U.S.)	Crackers Bread	Cooking, Sandwiches Snack	Mild, buttery, semisoft especially good in Tex-Mex cooking
Mozzarella (Italy)	Italian foods	Cooking Pizza	Semisoft, delicate, mild, white
Muenster (Germany)	Crackers Bread	Sandwiches Snack	Semisoft, mild to mellow
Parmesan (Italy)	Italian foods	Cooking	Hard, brittle, sharp, light yellow
Port Salut (France)	Fresh fruit Crackers	Dessert Snack	Buttery, semisoft
Provolone (Italy)	Italian foods	Cooking Dessert	Salty, smoky, mild to sharp, hard
Ricotta (Italy)	Italian foods	Cooking Fillings	Soft, creamy, bland, white
Romano (Italy)	Italian foods	Cooking	Pungent, hard, good for grating
Roquefort (France)	Bland crackers Fresh fruit	Dips, Salads Dessert	Semisoft, sharp, blue-veined, crumbly
Stilton (England)	Fresh fruit Bland crackers	Dips, Salads Dessert	Semisoft, sharp, blue-veined
Swiss (Switzerland)	Fresh fruit French bread	Cooking, Snack Sandwiches	Sweetish, nutty, holes, pale yellow

Substitution Chart

Instead of	Use
Baking	
1 teaspoon baking powder	1/4 teaspoon baking soda plus 1/2 teaspoon cream of tartar
1 tablespoon cornstarch (for thickening)	2 tablespoons flour or 1 tablespoon tapioca
1 cup sifted all-purpose flour	1 cup plus 2 tablespoons sifted cake flour
1 cup sifted cake flour	1 cup minus 2 tablespoons sifted all-purpose flour
Bread Crumbs	
1 cup dry bread crumbs	3/4 cup cracker crumbs
Dairy	
1 cup buttermilk	1 cup sour milk or 1 cup yogurt
1 cup heavy cream	3/4 cup milk plus 1/3 cup butter
1 cup light cream	7/8 cup skim milk plus 3 tablespoons butter
1 cup sour cream	7/8 cup sour milk plus 3 tablespoons butter
1 cup sour milk	1 cup milk plus 1 tablespoon vinegar or lemon juice or 1 cup buttermilk
Seasoning	
1 teaspoon allspice	1/2 teaspoon cinnamon plus 1/8 teaspoon cloves
1 cup catsup	1 cup tomato sauce plus 1/2 cup sugar plus 2 tablespoons vinegar
1 clove of garlic	1/8 teaspoon garlic powder or 1/8 teaspoon instant minced garlic or 3/4 teaspoon garlic salt or 5 drops of liquid garlic
1 teaspoon Italian spice	1/4 teaspoon each oregano, basil, thyme, rosemary plus dash of cayenne
1 teaspoon lemon juice	1/2 teaspoon vinegar
1 tablespoon mustard	1 teaspoon dry mustard
1 medium onion	1 tablespoon dried minced onion or 1 teaspoon onion powder
1 teaspoon coriander	1 teaspoon cumin or cilantro
Sweet	
1 (1-ounce) square chocolate	1/4 cup cocoa plus 1 teaspoon shortening
1 2/3 ounces semisweet chocolate	1 ounce unsweetened chocolate plus 4 teaspoons granulated sugar
1 cup honey	1 to 1 1/4 cups sugar plus 1/4 cup liquid or 1 cup corn syrup or molasses
1 cup granulated sugar	1 cup packed brown sugar or 1 cup corn syrup, molasses or honey minus 1/4 cup liquid

Maximum Storage Times

Food	Refrigerator (36 to 40° F)	Freezer (0° F or lower)*
Meat		
Beef	3 to 5 days	6 to 12 months
Pork	3 to 5 days	3 to 4 months
Ground Meats	1 to 2 days	3 to 4 months
Ham	3 to 5 days	1 to 2 months
Bacon	7 days	1 month
Frankfurters	7 days	1 to 2 months
Fresh Pork Sausage	1 to 2 days	1 to 2 months
Luncheon Meats	3 to 5 days	1 to 2 months
Lamb	3 to 5 days	6 to 9 months
Veal	3 to 5 days	4 to 8 months
Variety Meats	1 to 2 days	3 to 4 months
Cooked Meats	3 to 4 days	2 to 3 months
Poultry		
Chicken, whole	1 to 2 days	9 months
Chicken, pieces	1 to 2 days	9 months
Turkey, whole	1 to 2 days (thawed)	12 months
Poultry, cooked (without liquid)	3 to 4 days	1 month
Fish		
All types	1 to 2 days	2 to 3 months
Eggs		
Whole eggs	4 weeks	9 to 12 months
Whites	7 days	9 to 12 months
Yolks	2 to 3 days	9 to 12 months
Cheese		
Hard cheese	Several months	6 months
Soft cheese	2 weeks	4 months
Cottage cheese	5 days	Do not freeze
Ice cream, sherbet, frozen yogurt		1 to 3 months
Butter	7 days	3 to 6 months
Vegetables		9 to 12 months

Maximum Storage Times

Food	Refrigerator (36 to 40° F)	Freezer (0° F or lower)*
Breads		
Quick		2 to 4 months
Yeast		6 to 8 months
Cakes and Cookies		
Baked cakes and cookies (without frosting)		4 to 8 months
Cheesecakes		4 to 6 months
Cookie dough		2 to 4 months
Pastries		
Unbaked pie shells		2 to 3 months
Unbaked fruit pies		6 to 8 months
Baked fruit pies		2 to 4 months

*The type of freezer, amount of food stored and how often the freezer is opened affect the quality of frozen foods. These are only guidelines. Assuming that foods have stayed solidly frozen for the duration of storage, quality will deteriorate, but safety will not be compromised.

Preparing Food for Storage

- Keep all utensils and counters clean. And make sure that cooked meat or poultry doesn't touch equipment used for raw meat.
- Cover and chill or freeze cooked foods and leftovers promptly. For freezing, use moisture-vaporproof materials such as freezer paper or heavy foil, or freezer containers.
- Store fresh fruits and vegetables in the refrigerator crisper. Keep items such as potatoes and dry onions in a cool, well ventilated place.
- Chill meat and poultry as purchased in clear packaging. To freeze, remove the clear packaging; wrap tightly in moisture-vaporproof material. Tightly wrap fresh fish in moisture-vaporproof material before freezing or refrigerating.
- Keep eggs in the covered egg carton in the refrigerator. You can chill leftover separated eggs in tightly covered containers (cover yolks with cold water). To freeze eggs, break into a bowl, stir to combine, and add $1^{1}/_{2}$ teaspoons sugar or corn syrup or $^{1}/_{8}$ teaspoon salt per $^{1}/_{4}$ cup whole eggs (two whole) or $^{1}/_{4}$ cup yolks (four yolks). Egg whites require no additions. Thaw in refrigerator. Use within 24 hours.
- Store cheese, milk, and butter tightly covered in the refrigerator. Chill strong-flavored cheese in a tightly covered glass container.

Hints for Buying Meats and Poultry

- Examine meats for trimmable fat and marbling (the thin white streaks of fat that appear in the meat). Choose cuts with the least amount of fat around the edges.
- Check the "sell by" date on all meats and poultry and purchase the freshest product possible.
- If possible, buy poultry that has not been frozen. Poultry that has thawed in the meat case should not be refrozen.
- The USDA "Grade A" marking on poultry shows that it meets government standards.
- Make sure that the meat or poultry looks and smells fresh and is not filmy.
- The skin color of chicken is due to the type of feed used. Chicken with yellow skin is no more nutritious than chicken with pale skin.

Meats and Poultry
Comparison of Nutritional Content

3 ounces, cooked	Cal.	Fat (g)	Sat. Fat (g)	Chol. (mg)
Beef				
Eye of round	156	5.5	2.1	59
Top round	162	5.3	1.8	71
Round tip	162	6.4	2.3	69
Top loin	173	7.6	3.0	65
Sirloin	177	7.4	3.0	76
Tenderloin	173	7.9	3.1	71
Ground beef	244	17.8	7.0	74
Ground chuck	228	15.6	6.1	66
Ground round	213	13.7	5.4	70
Veal				
Shoulder	145	5.6	2.1	97
Sirloin	143	5.3	2.1	88
Leg, cutlets, breaded	175	5.3	1.4	96
Loin	149	5.9	2.2	90

Comparison of Nutritional Content

3 ounces, cooked	Cal.	Fat (g)	Sat. Fat (g)	Chol. (mg)
Lamb				
Leg	162	6.6	2.4	76
Shoulder	173	9.2	3.5	74
Loin	184	8.3	3.0	81
Pork				
Tenderloin	141	4.1	1.4	79
Center loin	196	8.9	3.1	83
Leg (fresh ham)	188	9.0	3.1	82
Shoulder	208	12.7	4.4	82
Chicken				
Breast, without skin	140	3.0	0.9	71
Breast, with skin	168	6.6	1.9	72
Leg, without skin	146	4.8	1.3	77
Leg, with skin	184	9.5	2.6	79
Turkey				
Breast, without skin	115	0.6	0.1	63
Breast, with skin	161	6.3	1.7	71
Dark meat, without skin	159	6.1	2.1	72
Dark meat, with skin	188	9.8	3.0	76
Ground, light and dark meat	195	11.7	3.2	59

Beef Cuts

Beef Cuts	Descriptions
Rib roast, small end,	is taken from the small end of the primal rib. It is a roasting cut.
Rib eye roast or Delmonico pot roast	is the large center muscle of the rib. All other muscles, bones and seam fat are removed. It is used for roasting.
Round tip roast, cap off,	comes from the hindquarters. It can be roasted if of high quality; otherwise, it should be braised.
Chuck short ribs	are pieces of layered meat and fat and contain rib bones. They are usually braised.
Chuck eye roast, boneless,	contains the meaty inside muscles of blade chuck. It is used for braising.
Chuck arm pot roast	is a braising cut taken from the fore end. It contains a round arm bone but is also sold boneless.
Round rump roast,	a boneless roast that is usually tied, can be braised or roasted.
Bottom rump round roast,	an irregular thick cut from the hindquarters, is used for braising.
Flank steak or London broil	comes from the tail end of the loin. It can be pan broiled or pan fried.
Chuck blade steak	contains the blade bone, backbone and rib bone. It is braised or pan broiled.
Chuck T-bone steak	is taken from the center or nearer the rib end of chuck. It is usually pot roasted.
Shank cross cut,	taken from hindshank or foreshank perpendicular to the bone, is used for braising.
Top loin steak	is a boneless cut from the short loin. It is used for broiling.
Porterhouse steak,	the best short loin steak, contains top loin and tenderloin. It is pan broiled or pan fried.
Pin bone sirloin or sirloin steak	contains the top sirloin and tenderloin muscles. It is broiled or pan broiled.
Rib eye steak or Delmonico steak	is cut across the grain from the rib eye roast. It is broiled, pan broiled or pan fried.
Top round steak or inside round steak	comes from the hindquarter. It can be braised, broiled or pan broiled.

How to Cook Beef Cuts

Entrée	Cuts	Cooking Method
Steak (marinated)	T-Bone, Top Sirloin, Chuck Eye, Ribeye Tenderloin, Striploin	grilling, frying
Steak (not marinated)	Tenderloin, Sirloin, Porterhouse, Ribeye, Top Loin	grilling, frying
Swiss Steak	Top or Bottom Round (preferably tenderized), Cube Steak	braising, boiling, frying
Traditional Roast	Sirloin Tip Roast, Eye of Round, Rib Roast, Ribeye Roast, Boneless Rump Roast	roasting
Pot Roast	Arm Pot Roast, Chuck Roast, Blade Roast, Cross Rib Pot Roast, Eye of Round, Bottom Round, Boneless Shoulder Pot Roast	braising, roasting
Stir-fry/Fajitas	Boneless Sirloin Steak, Sirloin Tip, Top Round Steak, Skirt Steak, Bottom Round Strips	stir-frying, grilling, frying
Kabobs	Boneless Shoulder Roast, Top Round, Top Sirloin, Chuck Eye Roast, Ball Tip Roast, Tri Tip Roast	grilling
Stew	Boneless Arm Steak, Bottom Round, Round Steak, Chuck Eye Steak, Boneless Shoulder Steak	boiling
Pasta/Green Salads	Any Roasts or Steaks, Sliced/Cubed	grilling
Hamburgers, Meatballs, Meat Loaf, Stuffed Veggies	Ground Beef, Ground Chuck, Ground Round, Ground Sirloin	grilling, frying
Sauces (Stroganoff, Bolognese, Marinara)	Ground Beef, Ground Chuck, Ground Round, Round Steak, Top Sirloin Steak	grilling, frying

Ingredient Equivalents

Many foods change measure when you crumble, cook, shred, or chop them. Use this guide to determine ingredient equivalents and to convert a weight or item into a measured product. Listed below are some common before and after measurements.

Food	Before Preparation	After Preparation
Cereals		
Macaroni	1 cup (3^1/$_2$ ounces)	2^1/$_2$ cups cooked
Noodles, medium	3 cups (4 ounces)	3 cups cooked
Spaghetti	8 ounces	4 cups cooked
Long grain rice	1 cup (7 ounces)	3 cups cooked
Quick-cooking rice	1 cup (3 ounces)	2 cups cooked
Popcorn	^{1}/$_4$ cup	5 cups cooked
Crumbs		
Bread	1 slice	^{3}/$_4$ cup soft or ^{1}/$_4$ cup fine dry crumbs
Saltine crackers	28 squares	1 cup finely crushed
Rich round crackers	24 crackers	1 cup finely crushed
Graham crackers	14 squares	1 cup finely crushed
Gingersnaps	15 cookies	1 cup finely crushed
Vanilla wafers	22 cookies	1 cup finely crushed
Cornflakes	3 cups uncrushed	1 cup crushed
Fruits		
Apples	1 medium	1 cup sliced
Apricots	1 medium	^{1}/$_4$ cup sliced
Avocados	1 medium	1^1/$_4$ cups sliced
Bananas	1 medium	^{1}/$_3$ cup mashed
Cherries, red	1 pound	2 cups pitted
Lemons	1 medium	3 tablespoons juice; 2 teaspoons shredded peel
Limes	1 medium	2 tablespoons juice; 1 teaspoon shredded peel
Oranges	1 medium	^{1}/$_4$ to ^{1}/$_3$ cup juice; 4 teaspoons shredded peel
Peaches, Pears	1 medium	^{1}/$_2$ cup sliced
Strawberries	4 cups whole	4 cups sliced
Vegetables		
Beans and peas, dried	1 pound (about 2^1/$_2$ cups)	6 cups cooked
Cabbage	1 pound (1 small)	5 cups shredded
Carrots, without tops	1 pound (6 to 8 medium)	3 cups shredded or 2^1/$_2$ cups diced
Celery	1 medium bunch	4^1/$_2$ cups chopped
Corn	1 medium ear	^{1}/$_2$ cup cut from cob

Ingredient Equivalents

Food	Before Preparation	After Preparation
Green beans	1 pound (3 cups)	2$^1/_2$ cups cooked, cut up
Green onions	1 bunch (7)	$^1/_2$ cup sliced
Green peppers	1 large	1 cup diced
Mushrooms	1 pound (6 cups)	6 cups sliced or 2 cups cooked
Onions	1 medium	$^1/_2$ cup chopped
Potatoes	1 medium	$^2/_3$ cup cubed or $^1/_2$ cup mashed
Spinach	1 pound (12 cups)	1$^1/_2$ cups cooked
Tomatoes	1 medium	$^1/_2$ cup cooked
Nuts		
Almonds	1 pound in shell	1$^1/_4$ cups shelled
Pecans	1 pound in shell	2 cups shelled
Walnuts	1 pound in shell	1$^1/_2$ cups shelled
Miscellaneous		
Cheese, Swiss or American	4 ounces	1 cup shredded or cubed
Eggs	1 large	3 tablespoons egg
Egg whites	1 large	2 tablespoons white
Egg yolks	1 large	1 tablespoon yolk
Whipping cream	1 cup	2 cups whipped
Ground beef	1 pound raw	2$^3/_4$ cups cooked
Boneless meat	1 pound raw	2 cups cooked, cubed
Cooked meat	1 pound	3 cups diced

Measurement Equivalents

1 tablespoon = 3 teaspoons
2 tablespoons = 1 ounce or $^1/_8$ cup
4 tablespoons = $^1/_4$ cup
5$^1/_3$ tablespoons = $^1/_3$ cup
8 tablespoons = $^1/_2$ cup
12 tablespoons = $^3/_4$ cup
16 tablespoons = 1 cup
1 cup = 8 ounces or $^1/_2$ pint
2 cups = 1 pint

2 pints = 1 quart
4 cups = 1 quart
4 quarts = 1 gallon
8 quarts = 1 peck
4 pecks = 1 bushel
1 pound = 16 ounces
1 fluid ounce = 2 tablespoons
16 fluid ounces = 1 pint
1 jigger = 1$^1/_2$ fluid ounces or 3 tablespoons

1 (6$^1/_2$ to 8-ounce) can = 1 cup
1 (10$^1/_2$ to 12-ounce) can = 1$^1/_4$ cups
1 (14 to 16-ounce) can = 1$^3/_4$ cups
1 (16 to 17-ounce) can = 2 cups
1 (18 to 20-ounce) can = 2$^1/_2$ cups
1 (29-ounce) can = 3$^1/_2$ cups
1 (46 to 51-ounce) can = 5$^3/_4$ cups
1 (6$^1/_2$ to 7$^1/_2$-pound) can or Number 10 = 12 to 13 cups

Conversion Table for Liquid Ingredients

Liquid Ingredients

Liquid Ounces	Milliliters	Milliliters	Liquid Ounces
1	29.573	1	0.034
2	59.15	2	0.07
3	88.72	3	0.10
4	118.30	4	0.14
5	147.87	5	0.17
6	177.44	6	0.20
7	207.02	7	0.24
8	236.59	8	0.27
9	266.16	9	0.30
10	295.73	10	0.33

Quarts	Liters	Liters	Quarts
1	0.946	1	1.057
2	1.89	2	2.11
3	2.84	3	3.17
4	3.79	4	4.23
5	4.73	5	5.28
6	5.68	6	6.34
7	6.62	7	7.40
8	7.57	8	8.45
9	8.52	9	9.51
10	9.47	10	10.57

Gallons	Liters	Liters	Gallons
1	3.785	1	0.264
2	7.57	2	0.53
3	11.36	3	0.79
4	15.14	4	1.06
5	18.93	5	1.32
6	22.71	6	1.59
7	26.50	7	1.85
8	30.28	8	2.11
9	34.07	9	2.38
10	37.86	10	2.74

Index

218   *Index*

Bibliography

Betty Crocker's Great Grilling, New York: Macmillan, Inc., 1997.

Clingerman, Polly. *The Kitchen Companion*. Gaithersburg, Maryland: The American Cooking Guild, 1994.

The Great American Outdoors Cookbook. Nashville, Tennessee: Favorite Recipes® Press, 1995.

Herbst, Ron, and Sharon Tyler Herbst. *Wine Lover's Companion*. Hauppauge, New York: Barron's Educational Series, Inc., 1995.

Herbst, Sharon Tyler. *The Food Lover's Tiptionary*. New York: William Morrow and Company, Inc., 1994.

The Illustrated Encyclopedia of American Cooking. Nashville, Tennessee: Favorite Recipes® Press, 1992.

Rubash, Joyce, R.D., L.D. *The Master Dictionary of Food & Wine*, 2d edition. New York: International Publishing Company, 1996.

United States Department of Agriculture, various charts.

United States Department of Agriculture, web site.

Whitman, Joan, and Dolores Simon. *Recipes into Type: A Handbook for Cookbook Writers and Editors*. New York: HarperCollins Publishers, 1993.

Order Information

Hooffinfeathers

Mail To:

Hooffinfeathers Cookbook
P.O. Box 908
Charlestown, Rhode Island 02813
401-788-0766 • 1-888-CHEF-LN8

Please send _____ copies of *Hooffinfeathers* @ $28.95 per book
or two books for $43.90 (Savings of 25%) $ _____

Rhode Island residents add 7% Sales Tax $ _____

Please add postage and handling at $4.00 per book $ _____

Total Amount Enclosed $ _____

Method of Payment: ☐ MasterCard   ☐ VISA   ☐ Check or Money Order

Account Number _____

Signature _____ Expiration Date _____

Please print name and address clearly:

Name_____

Address _____

City/State/Zip_____

Daytime Phone Number _____ Nighttime Phone Number _____

Make check payable to: Hooffinfeathers

Check out our website at www.hooffinfeathers.com.

(Please allow three weeks for delivery.)